I always try to create
a calm and peaceful atmosphere
for the models we make.

MY 36 YEARS OF MODEL MAKING IN HONG KONG
King Y. Chung 鍾經洋

Published by MCCM Creations 2012
info@mccmcreations.com
www.mccmcreations.com
http://mccm.wordpress.com

ISBN 978-988-18583-8-2
Printed in Hong Kong

My 36 Years
of Model Making
in Hong Kong

King Y. Chung

mccmcreations

Contents

In a small way

My 36 years in architectural and product model making mirrors Hong Kong's own growth, development and changes over this time.

This book tells of an aspect of Hong Kong's recent history; the story of its remarkable growth in product design and manufacturing, urban expansion and the construction of buildings and infrastructure to support an economy moving from manufacturing to a more service and finance base. This is not a book showing how models are made — rather, it is a book that illustrates my life's work and puts that work in the context of Hong Kong's rapid development and its many changes in work, trade, society, housing, transportation, urban planning, art and culture, finance and economic structure.

My companies, KJAW Ltd and 3D Models Ltd, with a team of no more than seven model makers at any one time, have built models of countless landmark buildings and infrastructure, as well as prototypes and tooling models for various industries within Hong Kong, around the region and beyond.

Hong Kong is an international city, a melting pot, a gateway to mainland China and Southeast Asia, a cornerstone for trade, finance and professional services. As it has developed and grown, many of the world's established and rising designers and architects have come here to work and set up offices. It is a truism for many professions: to be the best you must work alongside the best, and at 3D Models we have been fortunate to work with many outstanding designers and architects and some have happily included our model making staff in their own project teams and considered them as full members, often working in their offices for the duration of a project.

Model making is part art and part craft, requiring a model maker to possess artistic flair, technical soundness, a good pair of hands and eyes; and, the ability to visualise and transform two-dimensional drawings into three-dimensional forms in a simple manner. A model maker must, calmly, endure meticulous and repetitive work and reproduce both an accurate representation of an object and a model that depicts that product in its best light. Finding this combination of qualities in a single person makes recruiting good model makers quite challenging!

Model making is a form of visual communication, enabling an abstract idea to be represented in a three-dimensional form. It is said that, "a picture is better than a thousand words",

"I believe that a model is better than a thousand pictures."

The techniques and processes for successful model making are the same whatever the product — a sailing boat, an airplane, a car, a telephone, a bridge or a building; to a model maker, the only difference is in the drawings.

A model is like a crystal ball: by viewing a model, an architect or designer can determine what works and what does not, what to keep, what to improve and what to eliminate in a design. Form and shape can be quickly realised by a good model maker, giving architects and designers considerably greater design freedom and avoiding potentially costly errors.

Models evolve during the design process as architects or designers modify and update their initial idea after seeing a 3D representation. Different types and scales of model are required; from 1:1000 scale concept models, through to 1:1 full-size prototypes. Models and prototypes are seldom kept — once made and having served their purpose in the design process they are cast aside; replaced by the real product or the actual building. Although playing a key role during the design stage, model making is unfortunately not considered an integral contribution and model makers are seldom credited for their role in developing a project.

Since I joined this industry I have seen considerable change in architectural and design practice — from pencil, paper and drawing board to computer, keyboard and screen, with greater utilisation of technology and Computer Aided Design (CAD) software. Computers have changed architectural design, larger firms are able to handle a greater volume of work and expand, while smaller practices without technical support have been superseded. Senior architects, brought up using a drawing board have come to rely on younger architects whose use of computers is second nature, and who can more easily do the actual drawing and rendering.

The use of computers, hi-tech materials and the latest structural and construction methods have brought greater design freedom, enabling the incorporation of complicated curves and 3D double curves alongside the more traditional straight lines and simple arches. This new technology has also enabled architects and designers to make more and quicker changes during the design process; all of which need to be reflected in the finished model. This has made life for a model maker more challenging — however, we have to keep pace with the world and so have evolved our methods to fit with a changing reality.

In this book, I have shown models of all our major projects, including the HSBC Headquarters, the Hong Kong International Airport, many MTR Stations and related infrastructure. Throughout the book are specimen Hong Kong banknotes containing images of the buildings and infrastructure for which we have made models — these projects appear on 30 of the 40 currently circulating banknotes; an indication of their importance to Hong Kong's development and society. A brief anecdotal timeline is provided below, placing our models in the context of Hong Kong's changing urban and social landscape.

The workload of designers and architects fluctuates. After a project is finished we frequently do not hear from a client for a long time, until they come back to use our services again. But for the past 36 years we have been providing our clients with a consistently high quality of service. We have maintained that quality by being selective about the projects we take on, and the clients with whom we work. Over the years our clients have come back again and again, as is demonstrated by the projects in this book.

While writing this book I went through old company archives — thousands of slides, negatives and photographs, reams of files and records — matching names, dates and model scales. After all these years, it was a difficult task, but if not done now more records would be lost. As I looked over a life's work, I realised how lucky I have been to participate in so many important projects — so many of the buildings for which I have made models will stand for the next 50 years and, perhaps, beyond.

King Y. Chung

Over These Years ...

1950s-1960s

I attended St. Stephen's College in Stanley as a boarder for seven years and with lots of free time, I discovered that I loved using my hands and model making. The most important lesson I learned at school was to complete a task immediately rather than waiting until later. So, now I do as much as possible up-front on a project, including thinking it through, so any 'surprise' is minimised. I failed so many examinations by leaving the revision of schoolwork until the last minute!

1968-1974

My first job was at Topper Toys, an American toy manufacturing company in Hong Kong.

It was at this time that I learned the core set of skills I have used throughout my working life. These include designing, creating hand samples, developing prototypes, working out ratios for gearboxes, calculating tooling efficiency, creating tooling models, tooling, quality assurance techniques and quality control. I also learned the importance of quality and that good quality costs no more than bad quality!

1974-1976

I moved from Topper Toys to King White & Co., creating a line of tin soldiers, both mounted and on foot. I also became proficient in the skills of creating hand samples, engraving, master making and white-metal casting.

1976

I obtained my first freelance professional model making project from Gibb Livingstone and Bogi Toys, who wanted a new line of toys for boys and commissioned me to make three hand samples. Using their deposit for this HK$7,500 job, I formed KJAW Ltd and worked alone making toy and car hand samples in an 8x10 foot work space.

1977

I established a joint venture company, Handcraft Models Ltd, with Authentic Shipmodels Amsterdam to explore new opportunities and train model makers to build high quality model sailing ships. We

stopped production of the sailing ships after four years as the sales turnaround time was too long and production costs too high.

1980

We purchased a lost-wax casting machine from Germany to make silver jewellery and bronze miniatures. I spent time in Switzerland learning the lost-wax casting process under the wings of a master caster whose expertise was casting gold and platinum watch casings and straps for leading Swiss watch companies.

1982

Following a changing market, we made prototypes and tooling models for electrical products.

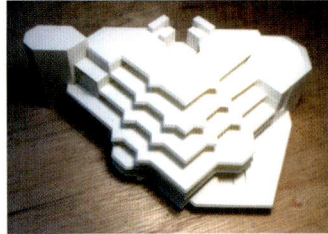

Our first architectural model was for the Hong Kong Jockey Club Sha Tin Club House. This opportunity opened new doors for my company, and as we had never made architectural models before, we were not constrained by old methods and techniques. We were the first company in Hong Kong to build architectural models entirely in plastic, giving us an edge over other model makers.

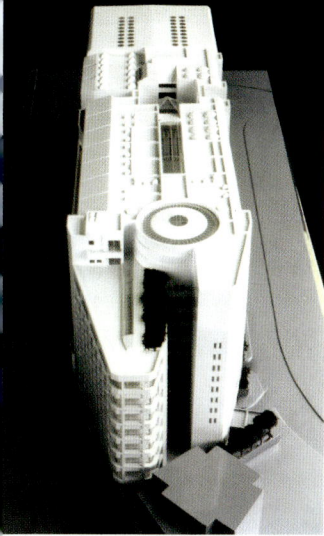

Hong Kong's population was growing with a consequent demand for public housing. The Hong Kong Housing Authority became the biggest landlord in the world and required a new headquarters, for which we made a model.

always recruited model makers straight from school and introduced them to the required work through in-house training. All my model makers could then work in a similar way with the same standard of work. This is crucial as a model is built in several parts and when put together must fit and look unified.

1983
We were chosen as the Hong Kong model maker for the HSBC Headquarters project by Foster Associates – this prestigious project established my company as the leading model maker in Hong Kong.

Foster Associates placed great emphasis on quality for all aspects of the project and our expertise in model making in plastic was one of the reasons we were chosen for this job. Other model makers in Hong Kong were, at that time, continuing to make models in paper.

1984
After winning the HSBC Headquarters contract, I placed a down payment to purchase my present workshop. In appreciation of Foster Associates and HSBC, I chose silver and grey as the predominant decoration colours for my workshop and company stationery!

Horse racing is a favourite activity for everyone in Hong Kong, whether they are rich, middle class or poor and consequently the Hong Kong Jockey Club's gambling on racing turnover is the highest in the world. In 1984, a new international standard racecourse was built in Sha Tin to cater for an increasing number of horse race-goers.

1985
My first overseas project was completed - Plaza Indonesia in Jakarta for HOK. This led to a range of other overseas projects during the next 15 years.

1986

Authentic Shipmodels Amsterdam moved operations back to Holland and Spain, and this joint venture ended. In recognition of the changing nature of the business, I changed the name of my company to 3D Models Ltd on 16 September 1986 with a headcount of seven model makers and one administrator – a number that we maintained for many years.

With a vibrant manufacturing industry, the Hong Kong Convention and Exhibition Centre was built to house the Hong Kong Trade Development Council and provide superb exhibition facilities to further promote Hong Kong industry.

1987

Hong Kong's container facilities were expanded from four to nine terminals and able to handle 55,000 TEUs of container movements a day – making it one of the busiest in the world.

A chance meeting with an electrical engineer who needed to make printed circuit boards overnight inspired me to enquire about photo-etching and, after learning the technique, we were able to make very accurate, strong and precise components before the use of computers and laser-cutting became widespread. Photo-etched brass parts can be nickel plated giving a metallic stainless steel or aluminium-like finish. Entertainment Building was the first model for which we used brass photo-etching.

During the late 1980s manufacturing and the production of prototype and tooling models began to move from Hong Kong to mainland China. I therefore concentrated on producing high quality architectural models and ceased other work.

1991

We worked with HOK on the Hong Kong International Airport Master Plan - a new airport for Hong Kong and one of the biggest projects in the world at the time.

1992

Foster Asia Hong Kong Ltd. won the Airport Terminal building project. We were asked to work with them on producing models for the project.

The airport's supporting infrastructure included the West Kowloon reclamation for the new Airport Express.

1993
Our models included the Tsing Ma Bridge; Central reclamation for Hong Kong Station; and, Sunny Bay on Lantau Island.

I was in the right place at the right time, and our company rode the Southeast Asian and Hong Kong property booms and the expansion of Hong Kong's infrastructure. We had the opportunity to work with top architects around the world and build many models for key buildings in the region and beyond.

Indonesia

Sri Lanka

Malaysia

The Philippines

Macau

Australia

Vietnam

New York

1997
On 1 July 1997, the United Kingdom handed back sovereignty of Hong Kong to the People's Republic of China (PRC).

The purchase of a laser-cutting machine and computerisation improved our operations.

Shanghai

Thailand

Beijing

1998
Due to the Asian economic crisis, our overseas work slowed, and I expanded the work we did in Hong Kong. An expansion of Hong Kong's rail system and the planned Tseung Kwan O Line kept us busy.

To continue being a logistics hub, Hong Kong needed to link its own road and rail networks with the Pearl River Delta, consequently Routes 9 and 10 were planned.

The Hong Kong Science & Technology Park was established for Hong Kong to compete at the cutting edge of technological innovation.

2000

I have always been encouraged by my clients to expand my business. However, to maintain quality I have kept my workforce small and lean. I used to compare my company to Snow White and the Seven Dwarves, as we had an office administrator and seven model makers, including me. The only difference is that we would work all day and get no play!

It is not the company that builds models, but its model makers. Many of my staff have served the company for at least ten years and some for over twenty. They enjoyed coming to work and going home at the end of a day knowing that they had done a good job. I do not agree with working excessive overtime. I believe working until 8 pm is fine, and that working till 10 pm is the maximum that is acceptable. However, working beyond 10 pm is not conducive to productivity, or safety and puts quality of work at risk.

Hong Kong's economy evolved to become a major financial centre and the consequent increase in office accommodation saw many office buildings being constructed.

2001

The integration of Hong Kong's two rail systems into one entity under the MTR Corporation saw new rail networks, new stations and interchanges being built; in addition, an upgrading of existing stations was undertaken.

Studies and proposals, requiring models, were completed for the controversial Wan Chai and Central reclamations.

The economic slowdown combined with cheap labour available on the mainland hit Hong Kong's modelling industry. Some model workshops closed and others relocated to the mainland with many good model makers being lost in the process,

and resulting in a deterioration in the quality of models made in Hong Kong. I decided to continue in Hong Kong with my team of model makers, maintaining my principle of not compromising on quality for price. I thought that with a population of seven million, Hong Kong should be able to keep seven hard working model makers busy, but it was not the case.

2002

At the end of 2002, I laid off all my model makers. Two agreed to work on an income-sharing basis, and we all hoped that one day when the situation improved we would be able to make a comeback.

2003

In the middle of 2003, the SARS epidemic dealt the final blow. With little work around, these last two model makers left to join an architectural firm and, with no work and no workers, I sold all my equipment and leased my workshop premises to this architectural firm.

Then, while the already laid off Snow White was tidying up accounts and I was tidying up loose ends, the phone began to ring again - first, Aedas called, then Arup, then Foster, then Rocco. So, teaming up with an ex-employee who had a laser-cutting machine, I was once again in business. By September 2004, the architectural firm, who had rented my premises and bought my equipment, found it too time-consuming to run their own model making workshop and terminated their lease. By October 2004, I had my workshop back and by leasing half, I marched on, just myself and my administrator.

2004

As Hong Kong wanted to become a centre for culture in Asia, West Kowloon was earmarked for art and performance facilities. I worked with Foster + Partners on the design and competition models for the West Kowloon Cultural District.

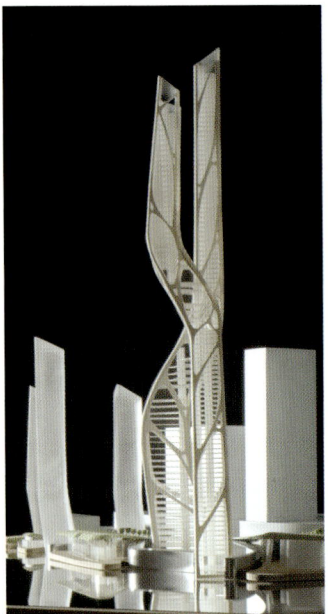

2005

With the collapse of Hong Kong's housing market and economic deflation, architects looked for work in the PRC and Middle East.

2006

Studies were completed to centralise the Legislative Council, Executive Council, Chief Executive's office and government departments at a new Government Headquarters on the Tamar site.

2007

Design competition model for the new Government Headquarters.

2008

Po, my brother and I learned sculpting techniques from Bryan Ellery, the British master sculptor.

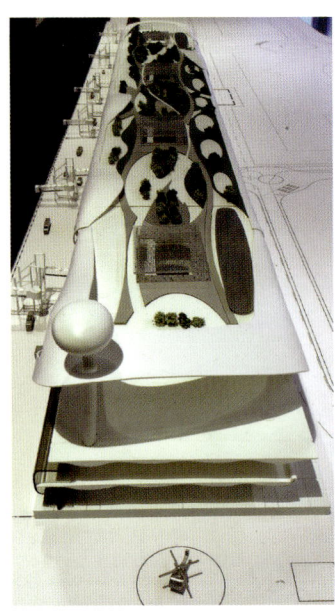

2009

A final decision was made to use the old Kai Tak Airport site for a new Passenger Terminal to accommodate large cruise liners.

2010

Between projects, I collect wood and tree roots as my new hobby.

2011
My personal assistant May Ling and I discussed the content of this book with MCCM Creations.

I started out in this industry 36 years ago as a one-man modelling workshop, and today I am back working alone. I can no longer take on large projects, but my many years of experience, my breadth of knowledge of the whole spectrum of model making techniques and the close working relationships I have built over a lifetime are considered to be of great value by my clients. Now, I only work for clients who know me well and who appreciate the high quality of my work. They happily understand the constraints as well as the benefits of using me for their projects.

I am still doing what I like most and what I do best. As this book goes to print I have completed 2,162 models and still continue to make the best models in Hong Kong and, I like to think, in the world.

I would like to say a big thank you to all who have helped me on my journey thus far.

HSBC Headquarters

New bank headquarters
for the Hongkong and
Shanghai Banking
Corporation

Foster Associates Hong Kong 1983-1986

香港匯豐銀行大廈

I was interviewed by architects Ian Lambot, Alex Lifschutz and Roy Fleetwood of Foster Associates in February 1983 — one month later we began building models for the HSBC Headquarters, our fifth architectural model project.

Bank Atrium 1:33 1983

On site, July 1983

People often ask me why Foster Associates Hong Kong awarded this project to us and I reply that it was because I told their architects,

"Trust me, I can do it."

There was a very limited choice of model makers in Hong Kong at that time, and I do not think any, including my own company, had the necessary experience to take on such a complex project. However, I believe our advantage was our technical experience in using plastic and metal to make models. In contrast, most other Hong Kong model makers were using paper in their model construction.

I was quite worried about taking on such a large project with just a handful of trainee model makers who, at the time, had little experience. However, with the help of young architects who were also learning, we progressed very quickly. Our work must have been good — Foster continued to use our services for future projects.

Partly finished models received
from Foster's London office.
We completed this model from
Level 0 to Level 13, including
the internal sun reflectors when
designs were available.

Link bridges – completed when
drawings were made available.

Level 0 to 7 and West Wing

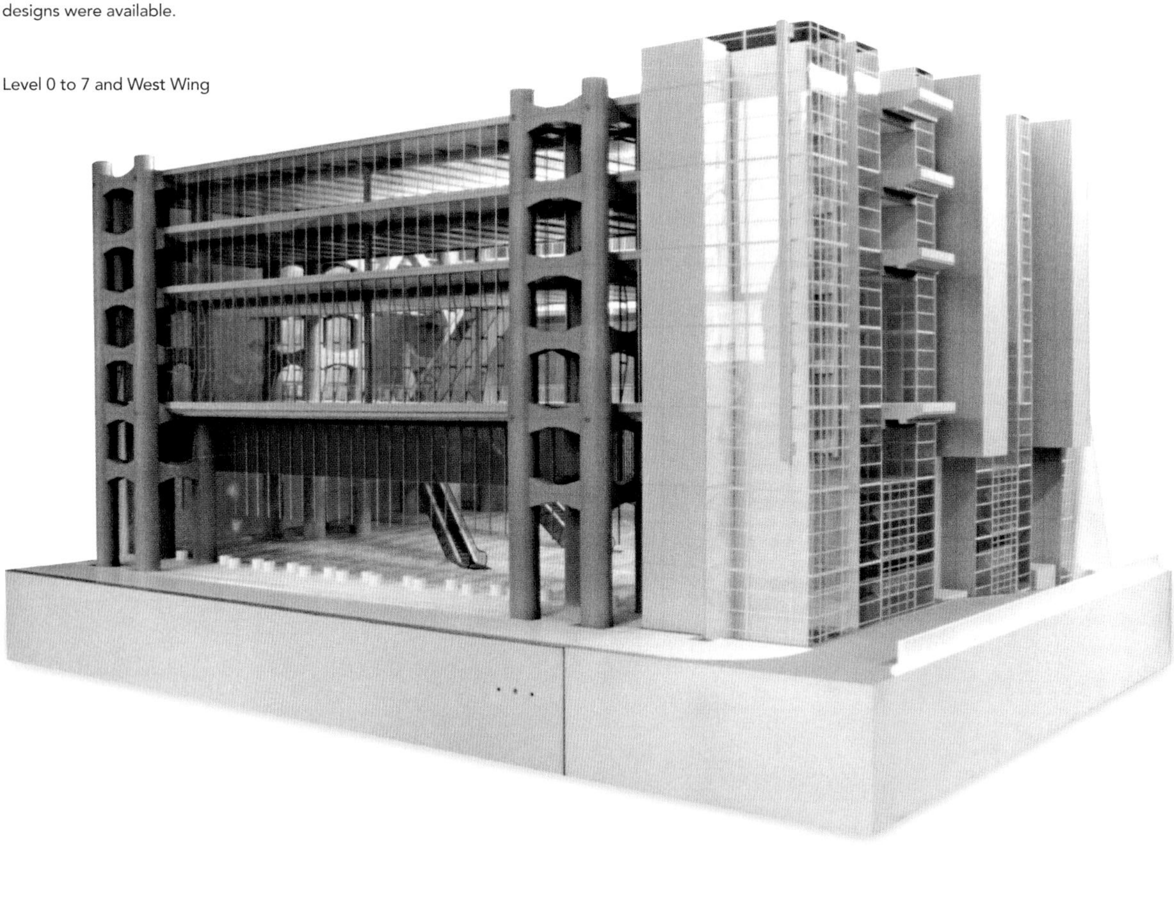

This was the first model we built for the Bank project. It was built in stages over a period of six months, and the whole model could be assembled and disassembled, allowing any part of the model to be updated independently of the other parts. This model was in an odd scale (1:33), all the dimensions had to be divided by 33 and the human figures, chairs, tables and computer screens were tailor-made for the model. It was built long before CAD was in common use, so we had to work with large piles of drawings and sketches.

1 Setting up the model for
   a photo session
   Level 0 to Level 13
2 Before computers and CAD
   were in common use, perspectives
   and renderings were difficult and
   time consuming to draw. By using
   a model, photographs could be
   taken from different angles.

I was told the building was grey because the model makers in the United Kingdom, who made the earlier models, started to build them before the final colour had been decided, but needing to spray the clear plastic with a colour decided, as an interim measure, to use the ICI primers P084-900 (white) and P084-700 (grey). After a while, people thought that grey was the final decided colour and to make the model more interesting three further shades were added — Construction Grey (a darker grey), Panel Grey (a lighter grey) and Silver Grey.

28   Looking into The Atrium and
        Level 3 Landing from East Wing
        1:33   1983

During a photo session, our team assembled or removed sections of the model to allow photographs to be taken of different sections and from different angles. Polaroid photographs were initially taken to check for angle and lighting; the set-up for a single shot could take hours. A whole roll of 36-frame slide film would be taken of an individual shot, as later copying of individual slides would compromise their quality.

Banking Hall Level 3 1:33 1983

A total of six different human figures were carved and two original chair masters made:

Female - sitting, standing and walking
Male - sitting, standing and walking
Chairs - With armrests and without armrests
The figures were duplicated by casting in white metal (tin + lead) using a silicone rubber mould; and, the chairs were duplicated by casting in bronze using the lost-wax casting method.

I returned to the Bank 25 years after the model was built and took a photograph at Level 0 at the same angle as the model photograph. I was surprised; the two photographs looked so similar, even down to the very smallest details.

1983 Bank Entrance / Typhoon Shutter
1:33

2008 HSBC Level 0 on site
1 Queen's Road Central
1:1

Underbelly / Level 0
1:33 1983

Underbelly / Level 0
on site
1:1 2008

Boardroom Floor Level 35 + 36   1:33
Models of typical levels
were built to support the process
of layout design.

Basement 1/ Bank Vault
1:50

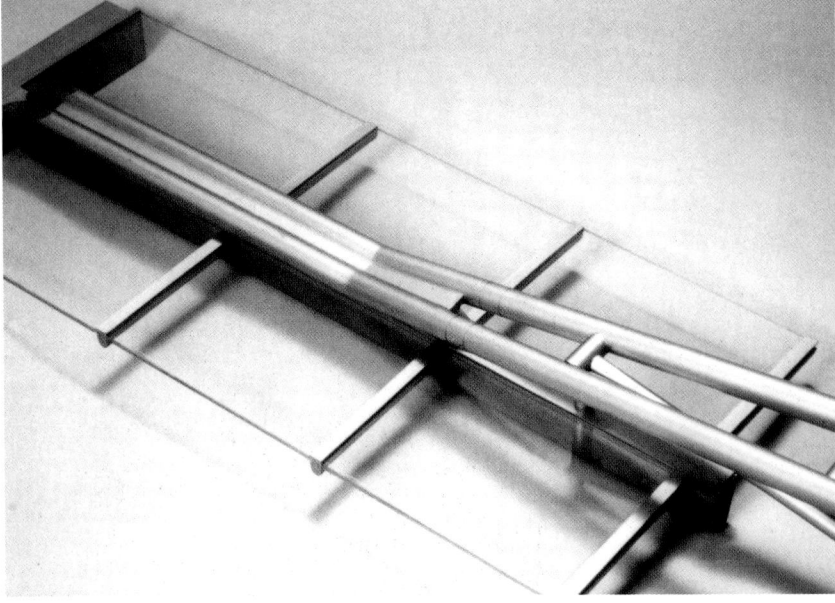

Underbelly truss 1:10
Underbelly hanger 1:5

Sliding Bank door on Underbelly 1:10
The actual model door can slide open and shut.

Models were built for many different parts and
components - some were rebuilt many times to
achieve the desired design objective.

Proposed external elevated walkway between
the Bank and Battery Path 1:20
This component of the design was abandoned and
an escalator was instead built between the HSBC
building and the Standard Chartered Bank building.

Crane 1:50
In this model the arm can be extended and retracted.

Curtain wall mullion 1:1

External Sunscoop working model. This model
had to include a movable angle: north/south to
follow the seasonal movements of the sun, and
east/west to follow the sun's daily movement.

Fire shutter on Fire Refuge Floor 1:20
In this model the shutter can be wound up and down.

Office Furniture and Appliances

1:10

Executive Offices

This model was loaned to each executive, so he or she could arrange the furniture to his or her own requirements. Photographs were taken of the finished model layout and used to position the furniture in the actual office before the executive moved in.

The metal parts of the chairs were made of sterling silver wire which was hammered, bent to shape and then soldered together.

Executive office suite 1:10

On site 1:1 1986

Foreign Exchange Trading (Forex) Room

We were also asked to make twenty actual workstations for use by dealers in the Forex Trading Room. We made special black melamine desktops, utility trays, speaker phone boxes, and cable ducts and assembled them with office manufacturer Herman Miller standard parts. Spray paint was ordered from Japan to obtain the required Nikon F3 black and red finish. The final commission, we believed, from Foster and the Bank began on 11 March 1986 and was completed in mid-June 1986. However, it turned out not to be our last piece of work — 22 years later, on 7 November 2008, Foster + Partners asked us to make a sample board for the Bank's renovation.

Cashier counter-top prototype

Sterling silver watch hanger
with adjustable length

1:1

Model making is serious work, but the circumstances and improvisations in which we need to work can lead to amusing situations.

1 Foster Associates gave us paint and thinner from Japan to paint phones and speaker boxes. The instructions that came with the paint stated that sprayed items had to be heated to 140°C in order to set the paint. So, we converted a steel filing cabinet into an oven by adding insulation, heating elements, a thermostat and a timer; put the sprayed items into the oven and heated them to 140°C. When we checked, we found that the phone boxes and speaker boxes were beginning to fall apart.

We had constructed the boxes using aluminium extrusions glued together with epoxy. When I checked the specifications for the epoxy, I found that to disassemble an item without damaging it, the item should be heated to 140°C. We were caught between a rock and a hard place! To address the constraints imposed by both paint and epoxy, we had to improvise by making jigs and clips to hold the parts together during heating, then, when the boxes cooled down, both the paint and the epoxy were set hard.

2 It was summer, and we had to work late into the evenings. On rainy nights, flying ants came into the workshop and shed their wings, which stuck to our beautiful, freshly sprayed paint. Even when we closed all the windows, the ants still found their way in. The only way to avoid the ants was to spray all the items before nightfall and put them into the oven before the flying ants arrived!

Touch phone boxes and speaker phone boxes

Hong Kong International Airport

The Hong Kong International Airport was built on the small island of Chek Lap Kok off Lantau Island, which after major reclamation covered a total area of 1,250 hectares and was, at the time, the largest civil engineering project in the world.

Making these models was a chance in a lifetime for us, and we knew that we would be able to secure this model contract because we had been working closely with HOK, the Master Plan design architect, since 1985. After meeting with Alan Bright and Ernest Cirangle we started the Master Plan models in early 1991. Two models were made at 1:2000 and 1:5000

香港國際機場

Hong Kong International Airport
Master Plan
Provisional Airport Authority
HOK 1:5000 1991

Airport Terminal Building
Foster Asia
1992 - 1997

In early 1992, I met Kent Lui and Chris Seddon of Foster Asia, who asked me to work with them as their contract model maker if they won the airport terminal competition. I agreed, since we had worked with Foster Associates Hong Kong on the HSBC Headquarters building a few years before and had established a good working relationship. I understood there were just three finalists, HOK, SOM and Foster Asia. We had worked with two of these three companies, so I believed the chance of obtaining a contract was quite good. Foster Asia duly won the contract, and on 11 April 1992 we began work on the Airport Concourse model; many other models followed, all completed to very tight schedules.

Foster Asia's three-point briefing to us for the Airport Terminal models was very simple:

1.2 metre grid; 36 metre span; Do not make it look like a warehouse.

This was the first model we built for Foster for the Airport Terminal Building.

3-bay Concourse study model 1:200 1992
In this model, the roof could be wound up and down to enable the architects to determine the optimum height for the Concourse. The Concourse height gradually changed from one end to the other.

2-bay Concourse with Shuttle Train 1:200 1992

Airport Forecourt 1:200

1992

Airport Forecourt on site 1:1

2008

After working on the grey HSBC Headquarters model, we hoped that Foster's Airport Terminal would be bright and colourful, but it was not to be. The Terminal was predominantly white, grey and black for the floors, silver, and blue, a colour commonly associated with the aviation industry.

Departure Hall 1:200 1992

Arrival Hall and Link bridge 1:200 1992

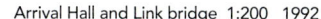

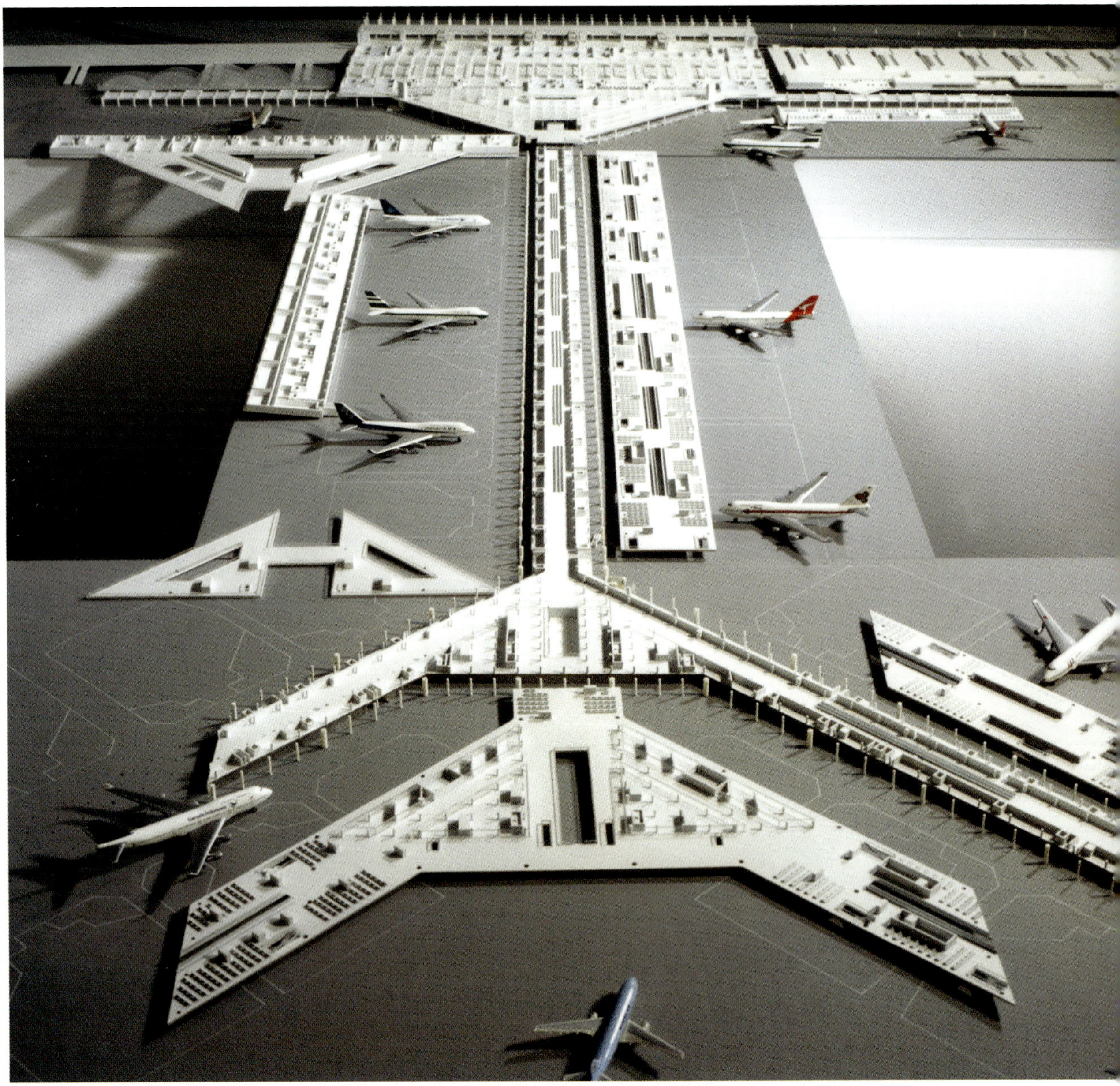

Terminal Building planning model with removable floor slabs and roof
1:500 1992

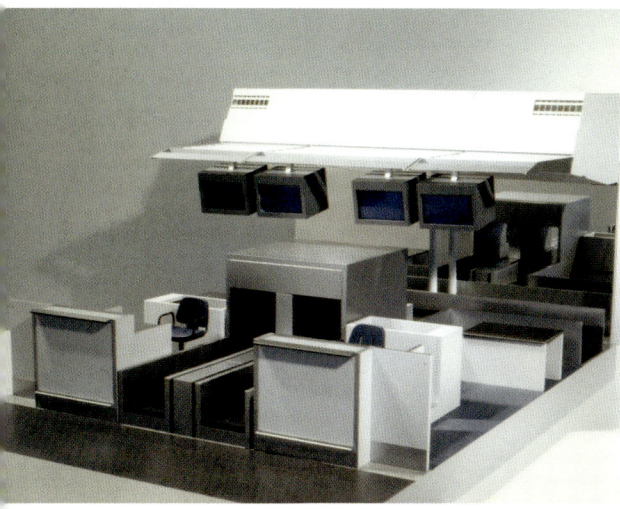

Check-in Counter
1:12   1993

Check-in Island,
restaurants and shops
1:90   1993

On site
1:1   2008

Ground Transport Centre

1 Link bridges between the Departure Hall,
  Drop-off and Airport Express
2 Airport Express structure
3 Airport Express
4 Column and roof

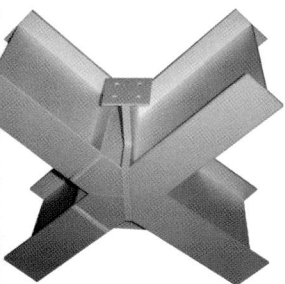

roof frame structure

1:1

3x3-bay roof with 9 different combinations of sun-diffuser and
maintenance catwalk
1:50   1992

linkage couple on site
:1   2008

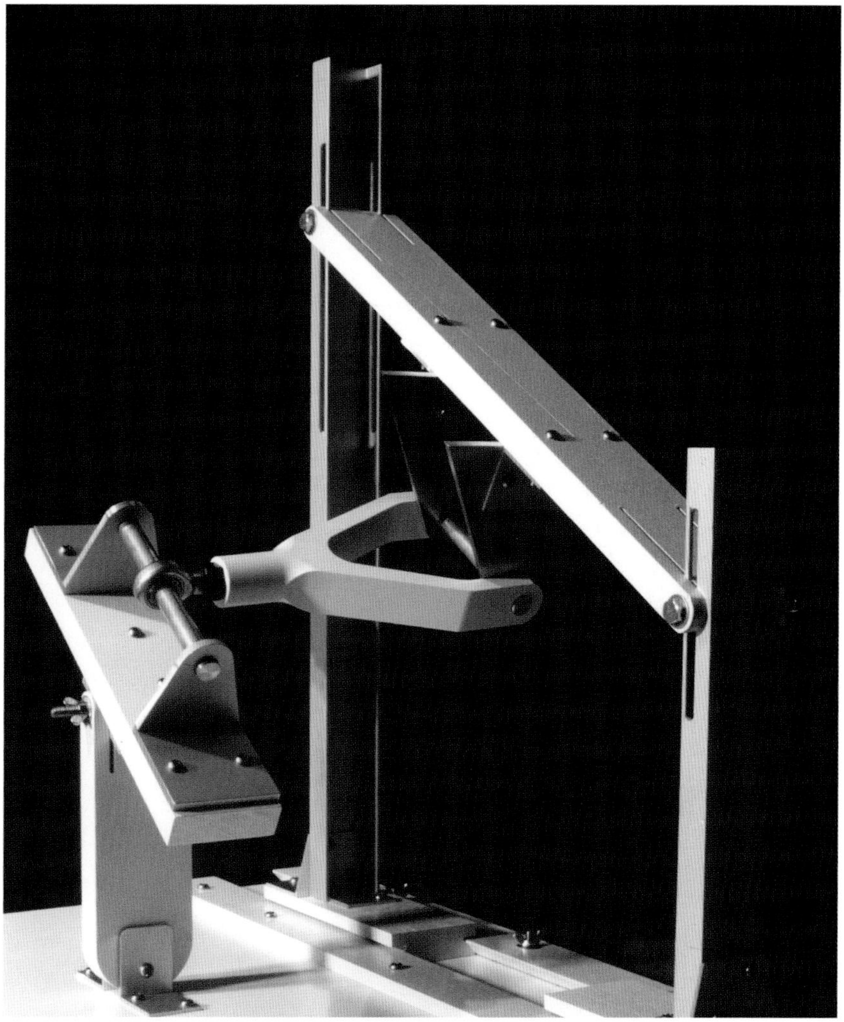

Linkage couple between the roof and the curtain wall. The couple allowed for:
- the rise and fall of the roof due to wind speed
- movement between the curtain wall and the roof
- the constant angle change of the roof arch
Ove Arup 1:2   1993

An airport links a city with the outside world, and Hong Kong International Airport required the construction of large road and rail infrastructure, including drop off and pick up points for buses, cars and the Airport Express system.

A pocket of land was reserved for future expansion: Sky Plaza and the new passenger Terminal 2 were built here, opening for operation in February 2007.

GTC sectional model 1:20
Airport Express Station – Ground Transport
Centre (GTC) 1:200
Advertising signage 1:10 1999
Airport Express rail and flyover 1:200 1994
Bus drop-off 1:20
Covered walkway 1:20
Future development site, road and rail for
Sky City (now Plaza) 1:2500 1998
Sky Plaza SOM / Aedas 1:500 2004

Kowloon-Canton Railway (KCR) / Mass Transit Railway (MTR)

深圳 Shenzhen

羅湖
Lo Wu

上水
Sheung Shui

粉嶺
Fanling

福田口岸
落馬洲 (福田口岸)
Lok Ma Chau (Futian Port)

天水圍
Tin Shui Wai

朗屏
Long Ping

新 界
New Territories

兆康
Siu Hong

元朗
Yuen Long

錦上路
Kam Sheung Road

荃灣西
Tsuen Wan West

屯門
Tuen Mun

荃灣
Tsuen Wan

大窩口
Tai Wo Hau

葵興
Kwai Hing

葵芳
Kwai Fong

荔景
Lai King

荔枝角
Lai Chi Kok

迪士尼線
Disneyland Resort Line

東鐵線
East Rail Line

港島線
Island Line

觀塘線
Kwun Tong Line

馬鞍山線
Ma On Shan Line

將軍澳線
Tseung Kwan O Line

荃灣線
Tsuen Wan Line

東涌線
Tung Chung Line

西鐵線
West Rail Line

輕鐵
Light Rail

博覽館
AsiaWorld-Expo

機場
Airport

美孚
Mei Foo

青衣
Tsing Yi

東涌
Tung Chung

香港
Hong Kong

上環
Sheung Wan

中環
Central

Guangzhou-Kowloon Through Train (Ktt)

The double-decker train runs between Hong Kong and Guangzhou.
1:87   1998

鐵路

大埔墟
Tai Po Market

大學
University

火炭
Fo Tan

*馬場
Racecourse

沙田
Sha Tin

大水坑
Tai Shui Hang

恆安
Heng On

馬鞍山
Ma On Shan

烏溪沙
Wu Kai Sha

石門
Shek Mun

第一城
City One

大圍
Tai Wai

車公廟
Che Kung Temple

沙田圍
Sha Tin Wai

九龍塘
Kowloon Tong

We provided models for stations (circled red) for Hong Kong's underground and overland railway network, including stations linking to the PRC.

鑽石山
Diamond Hill

彩虹
Choi Hung

九龍灣
Kowloon Bay

牛頭角
Ngau Tau Kok

寶琳
Po Lam

觀塘
Kwun Tong

坑口
Hang Hau

旺角東
Mong Kok East

藍田
Lam Tin

將軍澳
Tseung Kwan O

油麻地
Yau Ma Tei

佐敦
Jordan

紅磡
Hung Hom

油塘
Yau Tong

調景嶺
Tiu Keng Leng

54

East Rail Line (formerly Kowloon-Canton Railway Line) opened 1 Oct 1910
West Rail Line opened 22 Nov 2010

1 Lok Ma Chau Station RMJM 1:200 1999
2 2-bay platform at Hung Hom Station Foster Asia 1:90 1993
3 Lo Wu Station Spence Robinson 1:200 1985
4 Old Tsim Sha Tsui Railway Station 1:87 1992
5 Tai Wai Station 1:75 2001
   Interchange between East Rail Line and Ma On Shan Line
6 Interchange between East Tsim Sha Tsui and
   the Tsuen Wan Line 1:500 2001
7 East Tsim Sha Tsui Station 1:200 2001

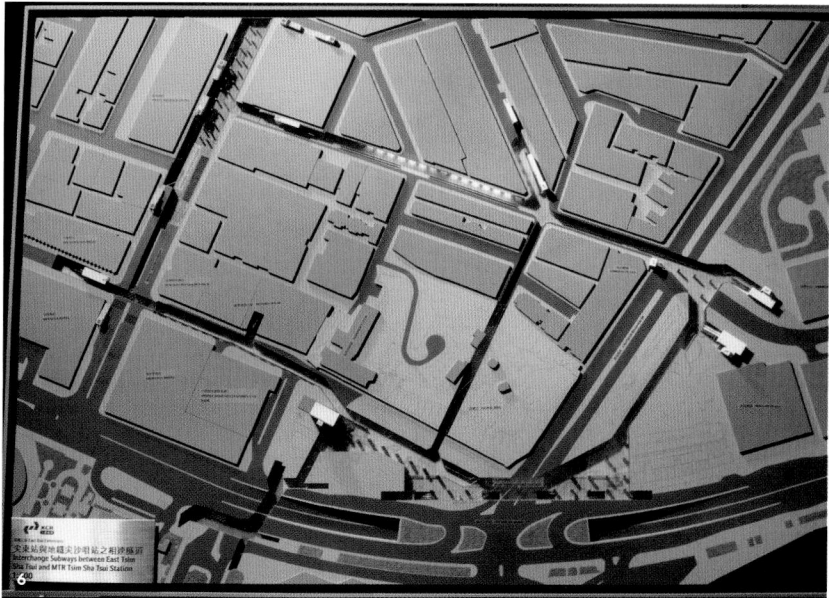

The old Tsim Sha Tsui Railway Station operated from 1921 until 30 November 1975, serving trains running between Kowloon and Canton/Guangzhou. It was demolished in February 1978 with only the clock tower retained. The old Hung Hom Station operated from 1975 and was replaced by a new station designed by Foster Asia in 1998.

By 24 October 2004, the East Rail Line was extended to the new East Tsim Sha Tsui Station, linking up the Tsuen Wan Line at Tsim Sha Tsui Station through underground passages. The West Rail Line currently terminates at Hung Hom Station.

Po Lam Station
RMJM 1:200 1998

Hang Hau Station
Percy Thomas 1:100 1998

Tseung Kwan O Line

opened 4 Aug 2002

Yau Tong Station
LPT 1:100 1998

Tseung Kwan O Station
LPT 1:100 1998

The Tseung Kwan O Line with five new train stations links the Kwun Tong Line and the Island Line. LPT wanted sectional models built for three stations in six weeks. We were able to meet this tight deadline by using AutoCAD and a laser-cutting machine to reduce fabrication time.

RMJM ordered a model for Po Lam Station and Percy Thomas ordered a model for Hang Hau Station. We made models for all five stations on the new Tseung Kwan O Line.

Quarry Bay Station
1:400 1997
Interchange between the Tseung
Kwan O Line and the Island Line

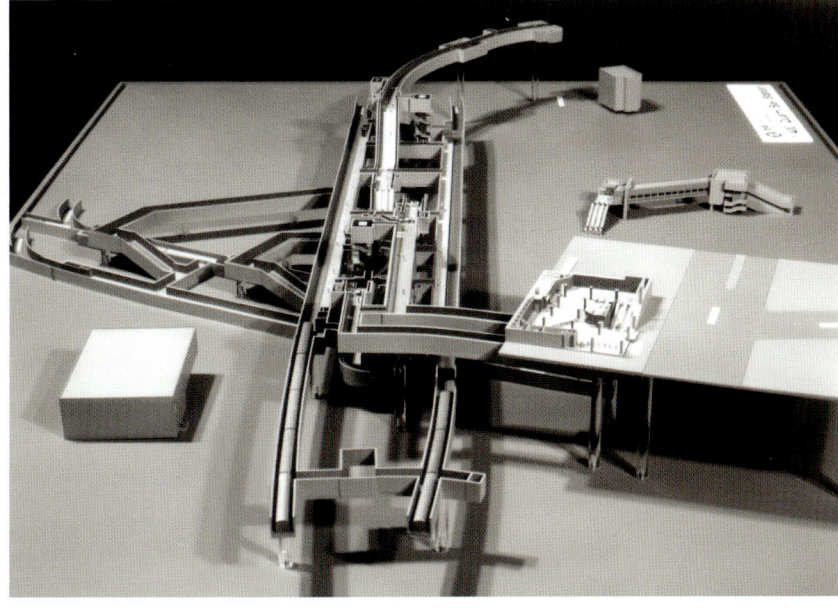

Airport Express opened 6 Jul 1998
Tung Chung Line opened 20 Dec 2003
Disneyland Resort Line opened 2005

1 Ground Transport Centre (GTC)
   Foster Asia 1:150
2 Hong Kong Station 1:200 2000
3 Sunny Bay Station LPT 1:200 2000
   Interchange between the Tung Chung
   Line and the Disneyland Resort Line

Ngong Ping 360° Cable Car opened 18 Sep 2006

1998

1:4000

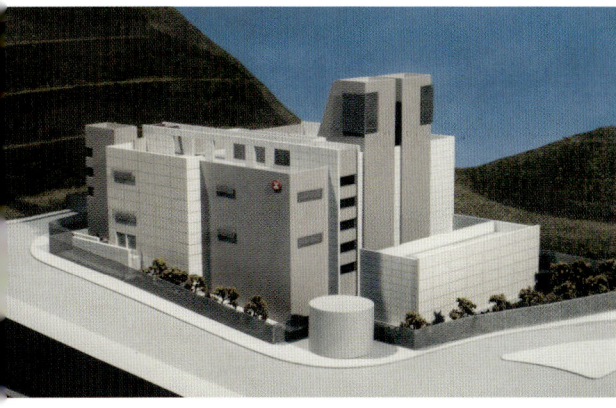

MTR Substations – supplying
electricity and fresh air to
underground tunnels and
stations
LPT 1:200 1999

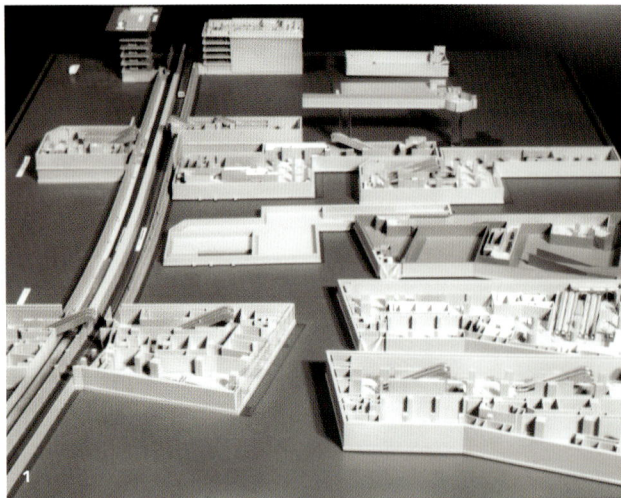

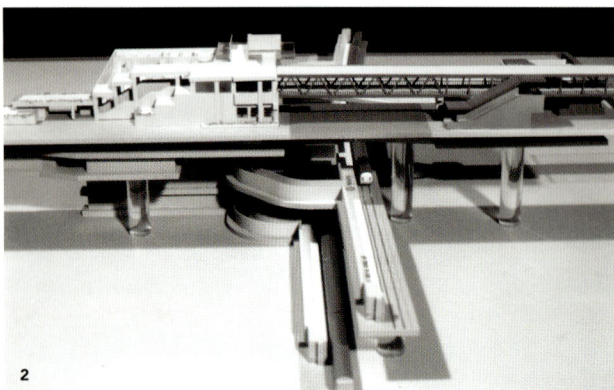

1 Sheung Wan Station 1:400 1997
2 Wan Chai Station 1:400 1997
3 Causeway Bay Station 1:400 1997
4 North Point Station 1:400 1997
   Interchange between the Island Line and the Tseung Kwan O Line

Island Line
opened 31 May 1985

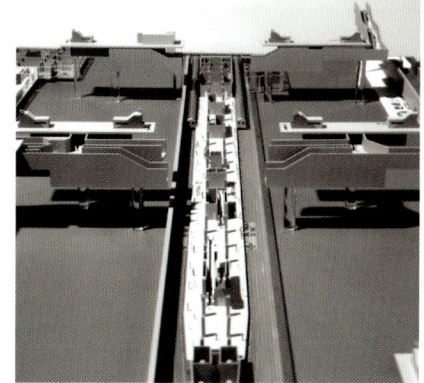

Mong Kok Station
1:400   1997
Interchange between the Tsuen Wan Line
and the Kwun Tong Line

Central Station
:500   1997
nterchange between the Tsuen Wan Line
nd the Island Line

Mei Foo Station
1:500   1998
Interchange between West Rail Line and
the Tsuen Wan Line

Hong Kong's MTR system is one of the most modern and efficient mass transit rail systems in the world. After 15 years of operation, the MTR Corporation wanted to extend, improve and create new underground passages and exits for many of its stations. We were contracted to provide models, but the piles of drawings sent to us for each station were confusing as many stations have areas that we, as passengers, did not know existed. We gained an understanding of the general layout and bearing of each station by cutting and assembling layers of cardboard, and then we started constructing the models. Each model can be taken apart to view all underground spaces.

Kwun Tong Line
opened 1 Oct 197

1 Tiu Keng Leng Station LPT 1:100 199
Interchange between the Kwun Tong Lin
and Tseung Kwan O Lin
2 Kwun Tong Station 1:400 199
3 Kowloon Bay Station 1:400 199
4 Choi Hung Station 1:400 199

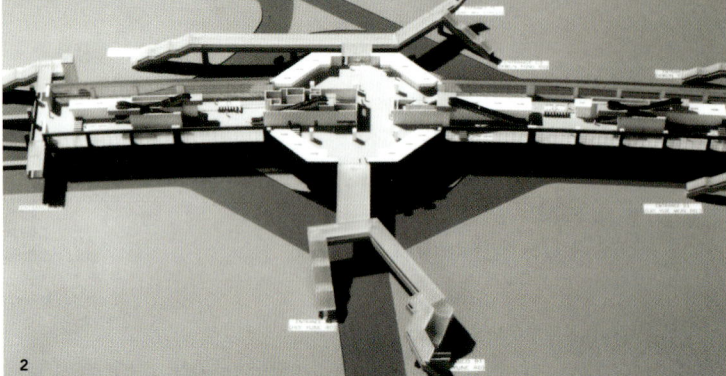

Kowloon Tong Station
1:400 1997
Interchange between the Kwun
Tong Line and East Rail Line

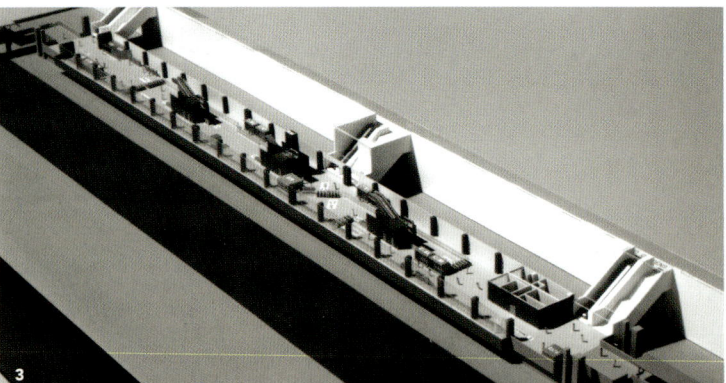

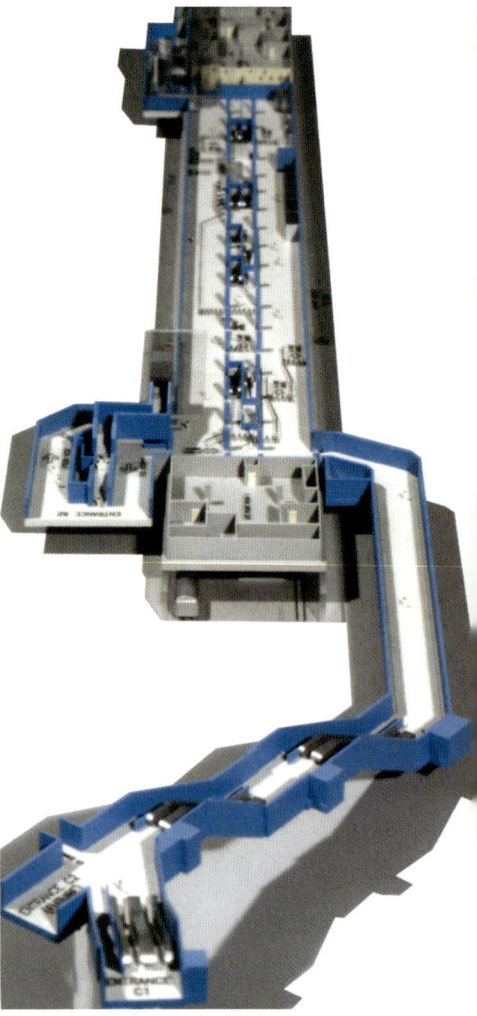

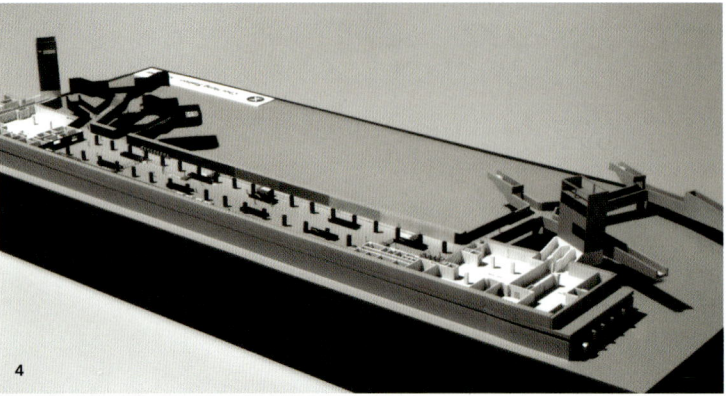

Glass Lift

MTR

1:8   1998

Lifts were added later to all MTR stations to cater for the disabled.
All structural parts of this model can be assembled and disassembled.

63

Kowloon Sky Rail

Hong Kong SAR
Hackett & Griffiths
1:90   1990

Kowloon Sky Rail — a proposed elevated rail system linking Hung Hom Ferry to Hong Kong China City, serving Tsim Sha Tsui East, Chatham Road, Salisbury Road, Star Ferry and Kowloon Park Drive.

Shenzhen MTR

Competition model Shenzhen, PRC
Integrated Design Associates 1:100 2000

Bridges
and
Tunnels

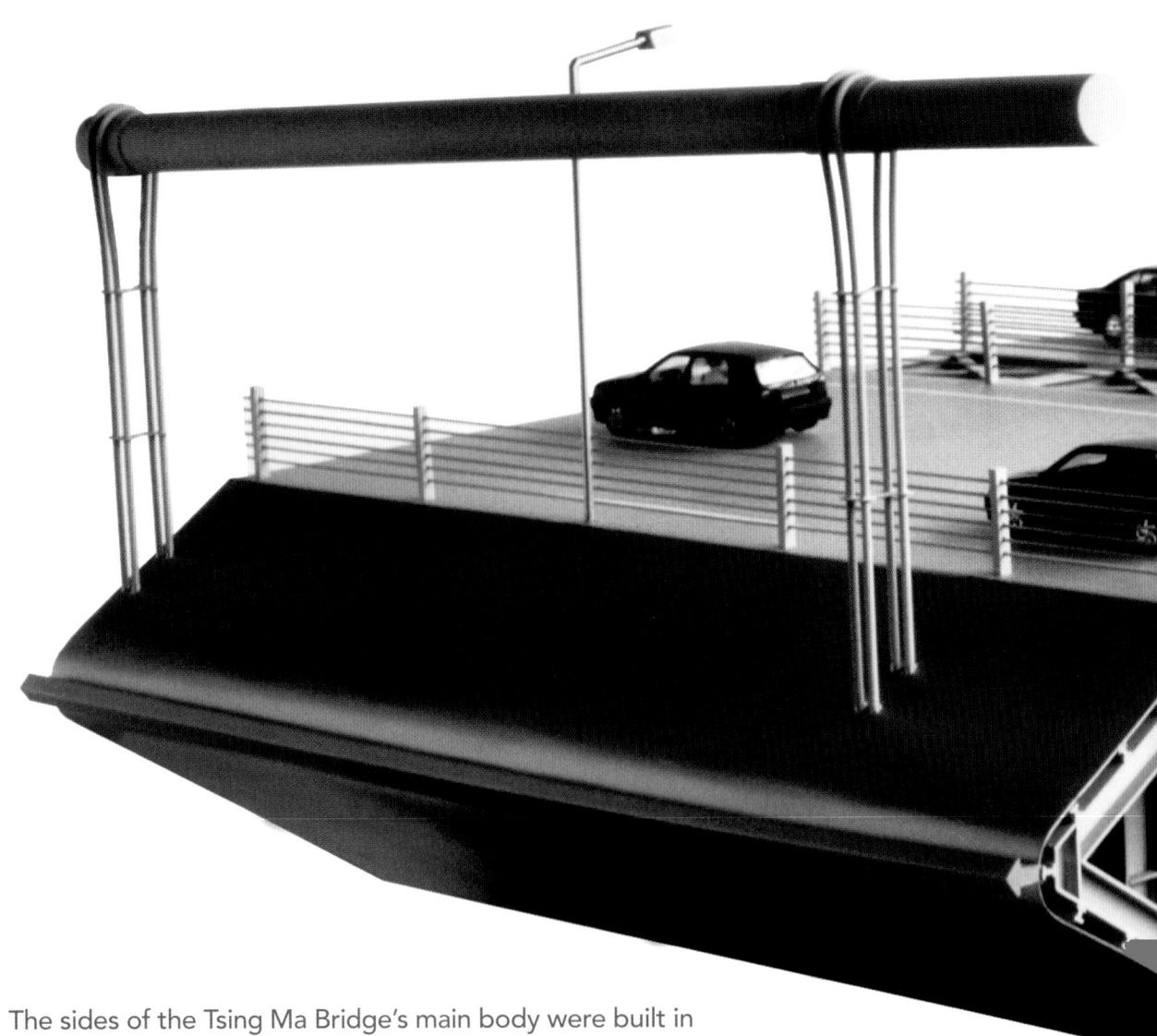

The sides of the Tsing Ma Bridge's main body were built in
a wedge shape to minimise the force of strong cross winds
that may cause the bridge to swing. The lower deck holds
the Airport Express Railway Line and two vehicle lanes
reserved for emergency vehicles. During strong typhoons
the six-lane top car deck will be closed, while the Airport
Express and lower car deck remain open for regular traffic.

Tsing Ma Bridge

Typical bridge module
(1/2 + 3/4 module)
Hong Kong SAR
New Airport Projects Co-ordination Office
1:50   1993

Tsing Ma Bridge
opened 27 April 1997

Sectional structure 1:50 1993

The Tsing Ma Bridge, at 2,160 meters, is the longest road and rail suspension bridge in the world. It consists of two bridge towers, 1,377 metres apart and 206 metres high, and 96 modules each weighing 500 tonnes, suspended from two one-metre thick cables. When I was a young boy, I always wanted to make a model of San Francisco's famous Golden Gate Bridge, but I did not know how to obtain the drawings. I was overjoyed when we were asked to make the model of the Tsing Ma Bridge!

Full length bridge
NAPCO
:1000 1994

The full length model of the bridge was weighed down with two brass strips to keep the main cables in tension. Screws and springs were added to the ends of the main cables; and, screws were used to adjust the tension of the cables so that the height of the bridge could be adjusted. Springs were used to absorb any vibration during transportation of the model.

Stonecutters Bridge

Section model
Hong Kong SAR
Highways Department
1 Option A Atkins China 1:100   1998
2 Option B Atkins China 1:100   1998

1

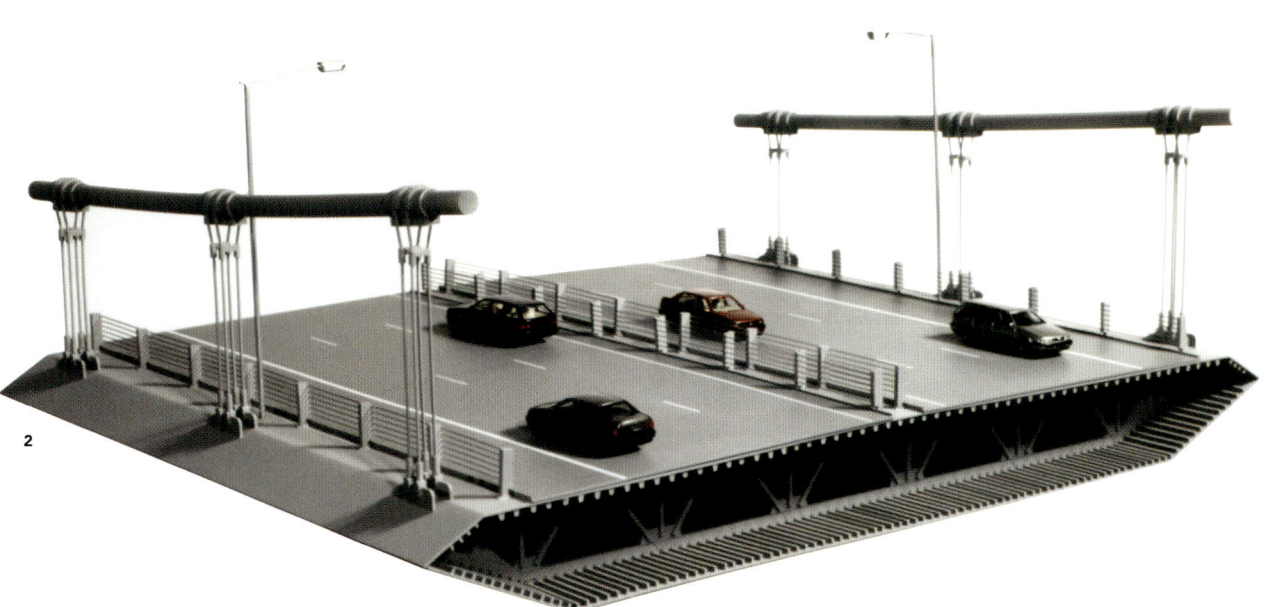

2

Tsing Lung Bridge

Hong Kong SAR
Highways Department

1 Option A Mott Connell 1:1000 2000
2 Option A Bridge Tower Mott Connell 1:150 2000
3 Option B Sectional 1:150 2002
4 Option B Bridge Tower 1:150 2002
5 Option B 1:1000 2002

Shenzhen Western
Corridor Bridge

Bridge Tower
Hong Kong SAR / PRC
ARUP
2002

1:150

Tunnel Boring Machine

Two electric motors were placed in the chassis of the model; one turned the cutting wheel and the other moved both paddles forward and backwards.

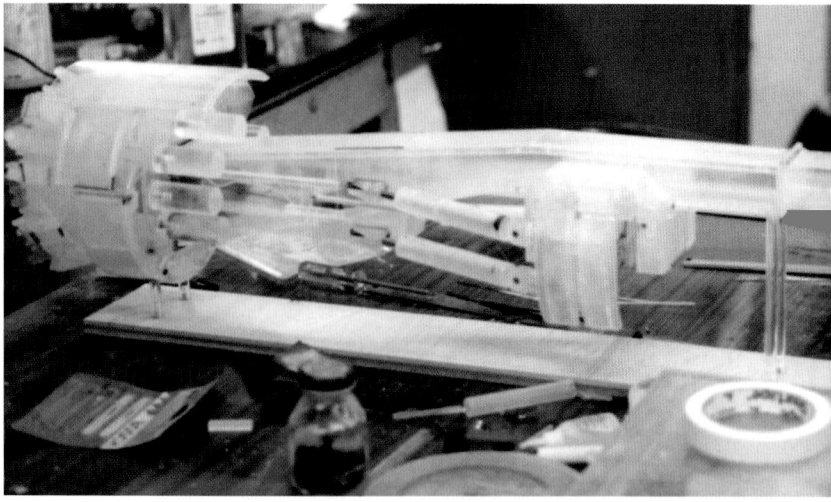

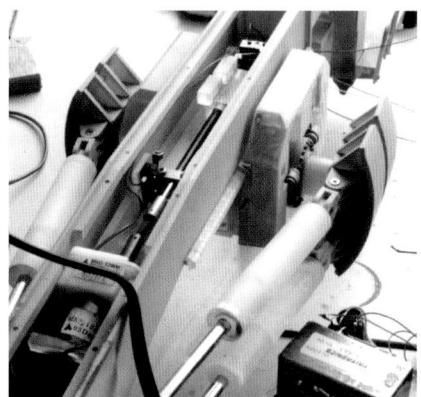

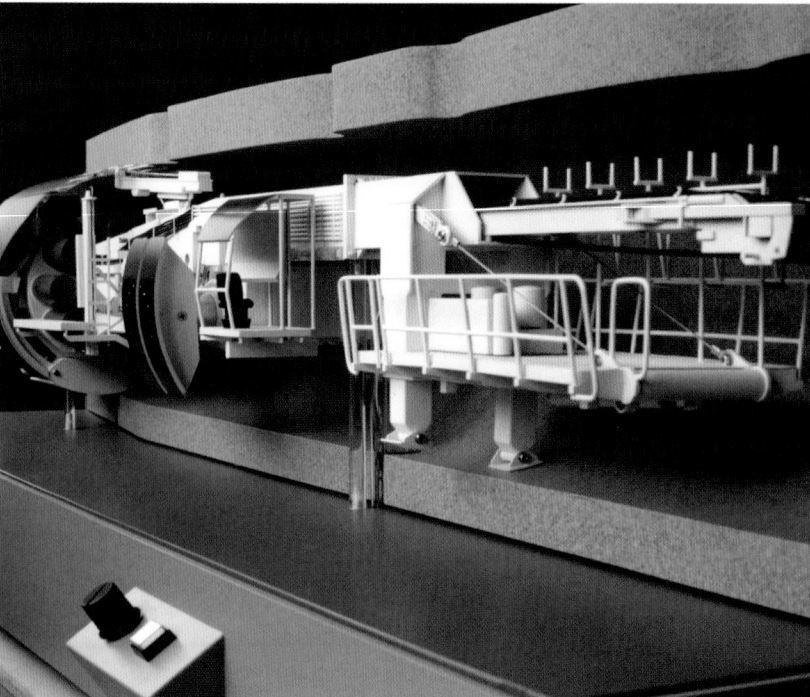

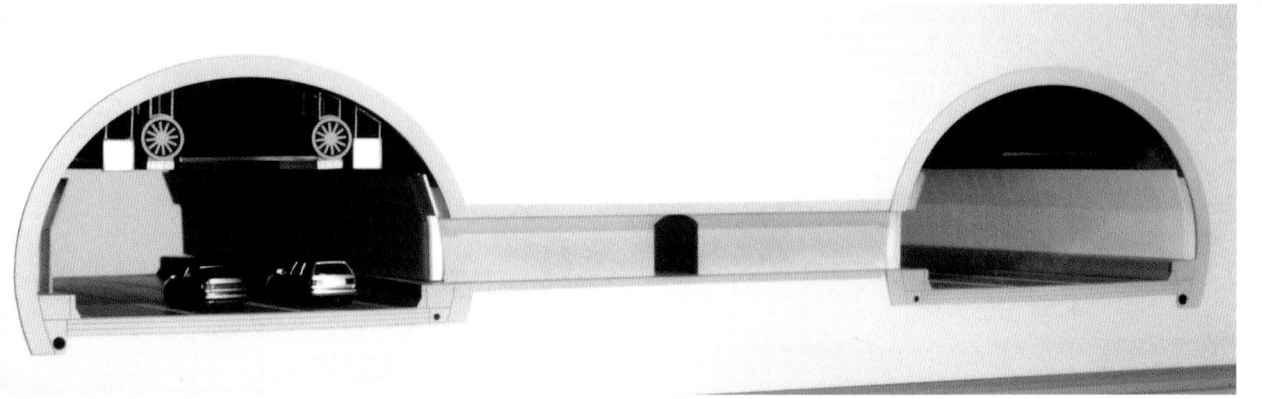

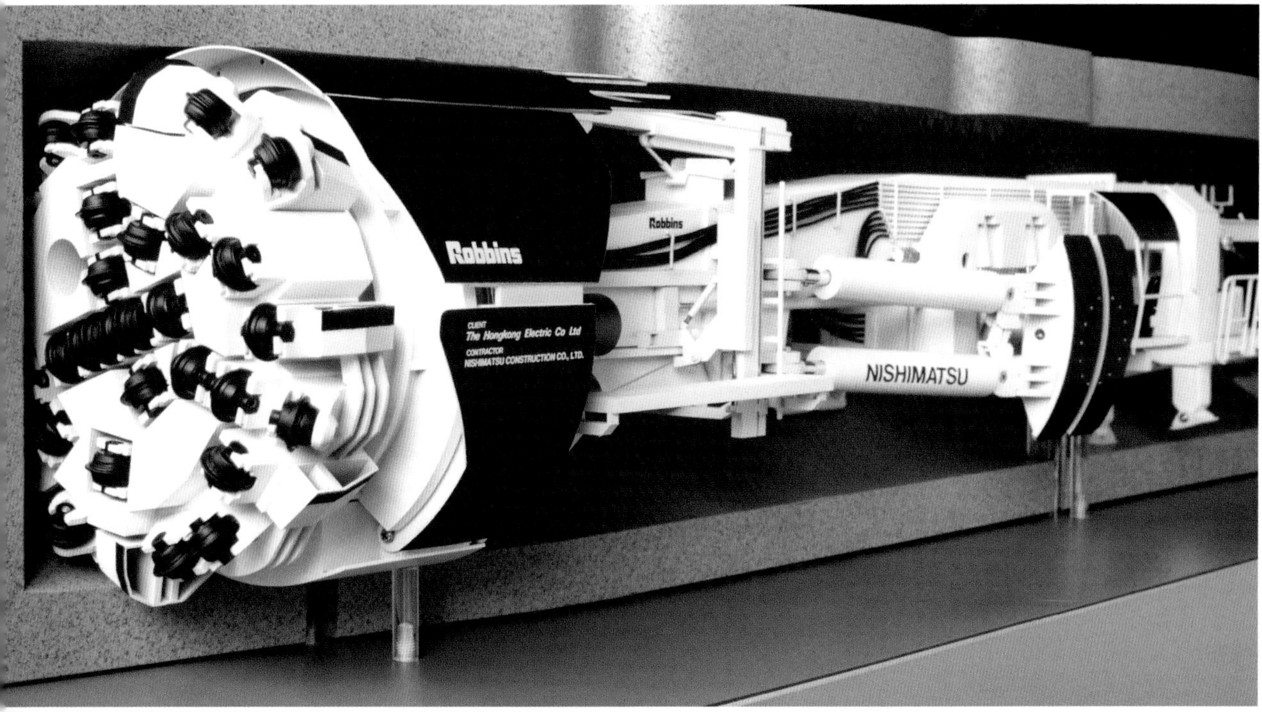

A Tunnel Boring Machine is used in many underground
construction projects. This boring machine went in at Chai Wan
Road next to Shau Kei Wan Fire Station and came out at Nam
Fung Road opposite South Island School, covering one third of
Hong Kong Island's length. The resulting tunnel holds electric
cabling from Lamma Island Power Station to serve the Eastern
part of Hong Kong Island. This model was built for educational
and maintenance purposes — by pointing to different sections
of the model the machine operator was able to tell engineers
which part of the machine had malfunctioned when operating
underground.

City Planning and
Infrastructure

Hong Kong

Central / Wan Chai / Victoria Harbour
LPT 1:2000 1998

This model depicts Hong Kong's Central to Wan Chai foreshore reclamation and urban landscape.

Kowloon to/from The Peak

(top) View from The Peak towards Kowloon
(bottom) View from Kowloon to The Peak

Hong Kong's spectacular harbour separates
Hong Kong Island and Kowloon and shows
the extent of reclamation and urban growth
over the last 30 years.

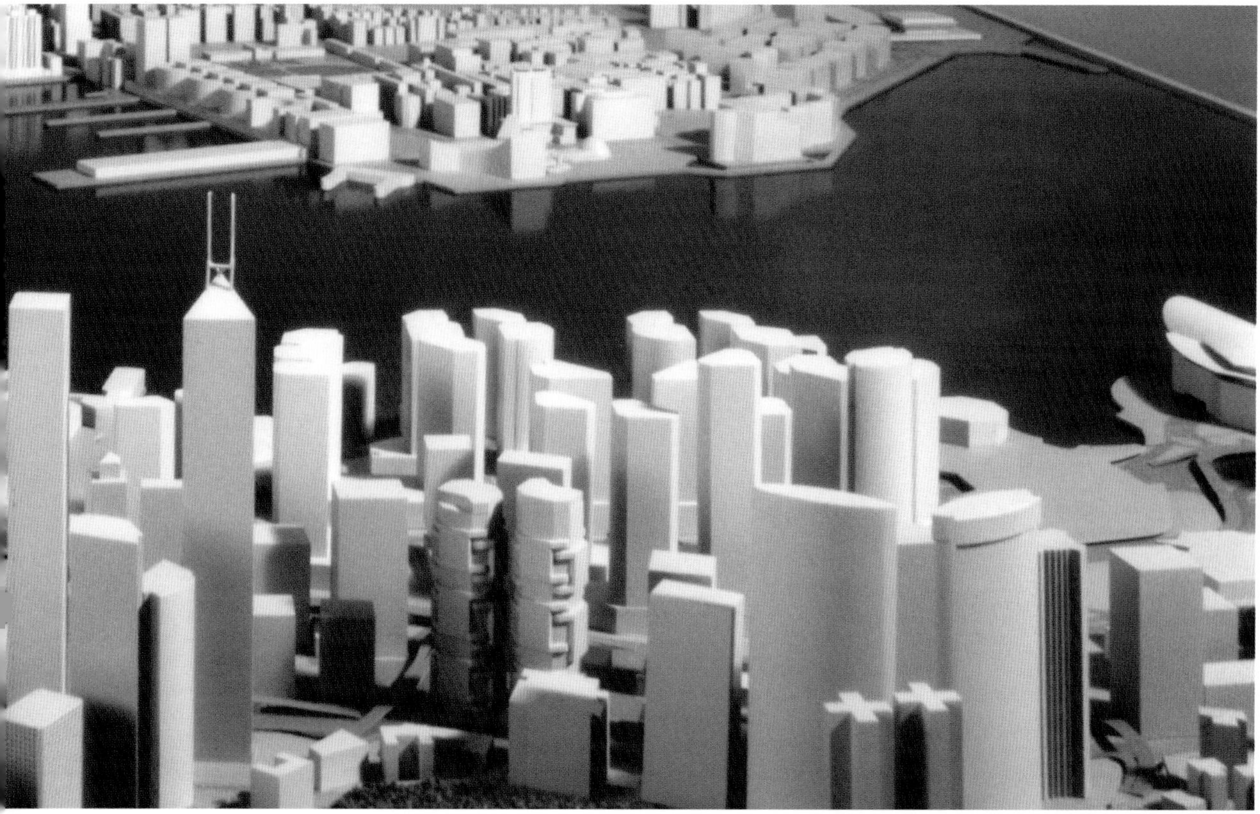

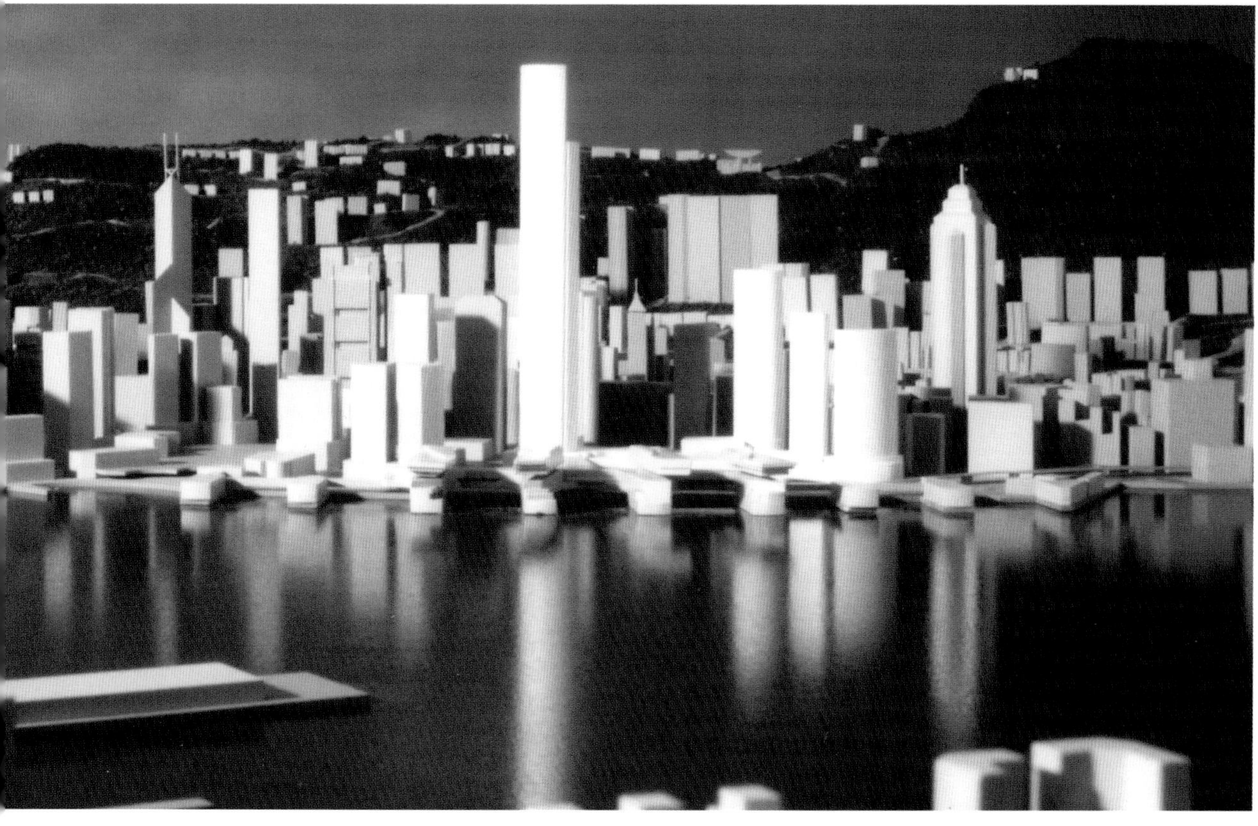

The Center

Hong Kong SAR
Land Development Corporation 1989

1:1000

Cyberport

Hong Kong SAR
ARQUITECTONICA
1000   2000

Kowloon West Reclamation

Urbis   (vertical) 1:1500   (horizontal) 1:2500   1992
This reclamation created new areas for residential and commercial
development, a link highway to the Western Harbour Tunnel and
rail infrastructure for the Tung Chung and Airport Express Lines.
The West Kowloon Cultural District will be built on the peninsula
formed by this reclamation.

Western Corridor

Urmston Road River Traffic

Ma Wan Channel

West Lamma Channel

Adamasta Channel

Kwai Chung Container Terminal
and Infrastructure

Hong Kong SAR
This 3D model shows Hong Kong's shipping fairways and
trucking routes. Over 200,000 ocean-going and river vessels
arrive in and depart from Hong Kong every year, carrying over
20 million TEUs per annum of container traffic.

Kwai Chung
Container
Terminal

Victoria Harbour

Lei Yue Mun

Tathong
Channel

East Lamma Channel

86

Terminal 3 MTL 1:3500 1987
Terminals 1 - 9 COSCO HIT
1:3000 1998
Mobil Oil terminal 1:200 1990
Exploded model to show truck
circulation inside the building
HIT LPT 1:250 1988
Hong Kong International Distribution
Centre HIT LPT 1:500 1988

In 1987, Hong Kong's container terminal expanded from
four terminals to its current nine; handling 55,000 TEUs
(twenty-foot equivalent units) of container movements a day,
it is one of the busiest container terminals in the world.

5

Route 9

Hong Kong SAR
Highways Department
Atkins China
1:5000   1998

Route 10

Hong Kong SAR
Highways Department
Mott Connell
(vertical) 1:2500
(horizontal) 1:10000
1999

1 Ferry Street Flyover 1:1000 1993
2 Noise Enclosure 1:200 1994

Sunny Bay

Hong Kong SAR
LPT 1999

Backup development plan in case of
an overflow of visitors for Hong Kong
Disneyland Resort, Sunny Bay on
Lantau Island.

1:1000

Macau

Nam Wan Reclamation
Macau Government
1:2000 1991

**Macau's
Reclamation
Projects**

One day, I took a call from a woman who said she was from the Macau Governor's office, and asked to speak to "Mr Chung." I replied, "I am Mr Chung, but I think you have the wrong Mr Chung. " She asked, "Do you build models?" I said, "Yes." Then she said, "Can you come to the Macau Governor's office tomorrow at 11am? There will be a return hydrofoil ticket waiting for you at the Macau Ferry Terminal ticket office." This was the start of Macau's grand land reclamation programme. Over the next twenty years, Macau's land mass doubled, a new airport was built and Macau was transformed into a gambling centre with revenue and turnover higher than Las Vegas, USA.

Macau

Macau Airport with Taipa and Coloane Islands
in the distance
Macau Government 1991

1:7000

Zhuhai West

PRC
RMJM
1993

1:3000

1:3000

Hong Kong Housing Authority Headquarters

1:250 1982

This was the fourth architectural model that we fabricated — it was also the first, and one of very few models that we worked on for a Hong Kong government department. Over time, I realised that government departments usually awarded their model making projects to the lowest bidder. Their terms for quotation and conditions of contract are quite stringent, and so, to minimise direct dealings with government departments, I decided:

1 That we would work for architects, civil engineers or consultants as a sub-contractor, once they had secured a project.
2 We would only bid for technical and specialised projects that other model makers could not or did not want, for example, bridges and structural projects.
3 We would bid for projects of importance.

Hong Kong Convention and Exhibition Centre

Hong Kong SAR
Polytown / New World
Ng Chun Man   1:200   1986

This model was built for the Hong Kong Convention and Exhibition Centre's foundation stone laying ceremony performed by H.M. Queen Elizabeth II.

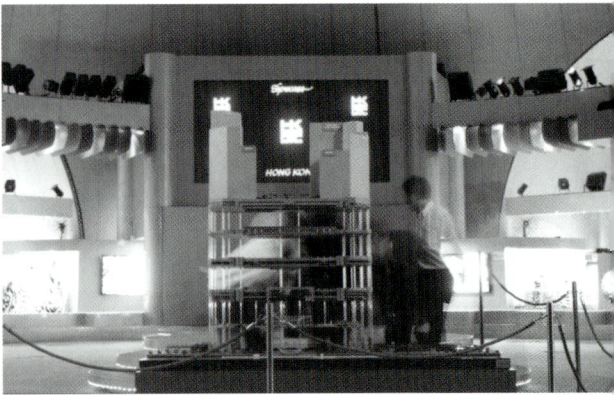

y using clear acrylic rods
 raise the floor plates,
 exploded model
as created with all
xhibition halls, theatres,
onference rooms,
ntrances and basement
ar parking clearly visible.

**Hong Kong Jockey Club
Sha Tin Racecourse**

The Hong Kong Jockey Club's Sha Tin Club House was the first architectural model that we ever fabricated, and although not complicated, was very complex for us at the time.

We had used engineering drawings before, but suddenly there were a whole new set of signs and rules that had to be learned and understood when using architectural drawings. I asked Terence Kiernan of Prescott Stutely Design Group what the different symbols meant. His "Oh, my God!" still rings in my ears! Anyway, he let us have the job and after quickly learning the new terminology, this was the beginning of our long adventure in the world of architectural model making.

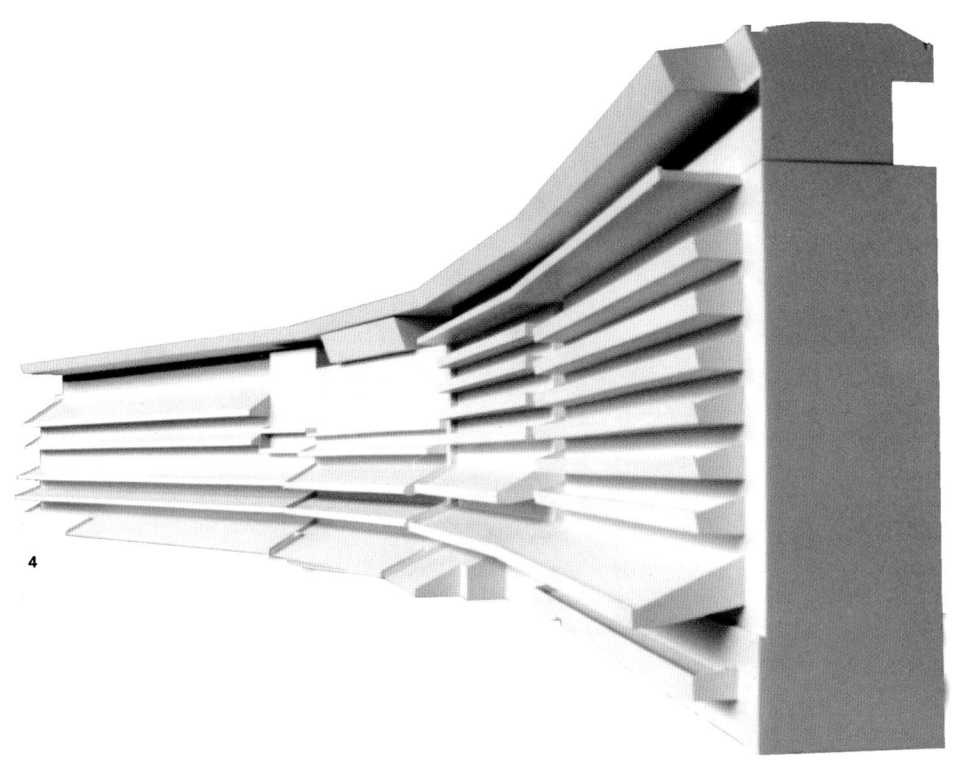

Sha Tin Club House
Prescott Stutely Design Group
1:500   1982
Sha Tin Club House
Prescott Stutely Design Group
1:200   1984
Sha Tin Jockey Club Race Stand
Leigh & Orange 1:200   1984
Happy Valley Race Stand extension
RMJM 1:200   1987
Shan Kwong Road Club House
study model
RMJM 1:200   1988

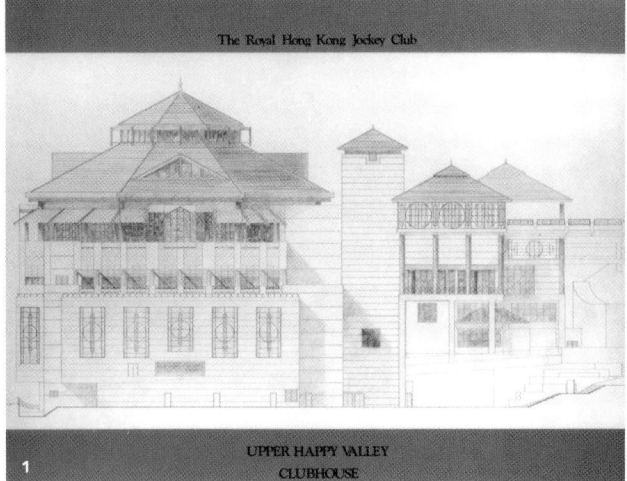

1/2/5 Hong Kong Jockey Club, Shan Kwong Road Club House RMJM 1:200 1991
3/4 Proposed relocation of Hong Kong Football Club House to Upper Happy Valley
Hackett & Griffiths 1:200 1988

**Hong Kong Science &
Technology Parks**

1 City Planning Consultants 1:1000 1998
2 City Planning Consultants 1:500 1999
3/4 Hong Kong Science & Technology Parks
   LD Asia / Maunsell Consultants Asia 1:500 2002

**West Kowloon Cultural District
proposed performing arts venue**

Hong Kong SAR
Cheung Kong
Foster + Partners
1:200   2003

**Hong Kong Government
New Headquarters – Tamar**

Pre-qualifying competition model
Dragages / Aedas 2006

1:750

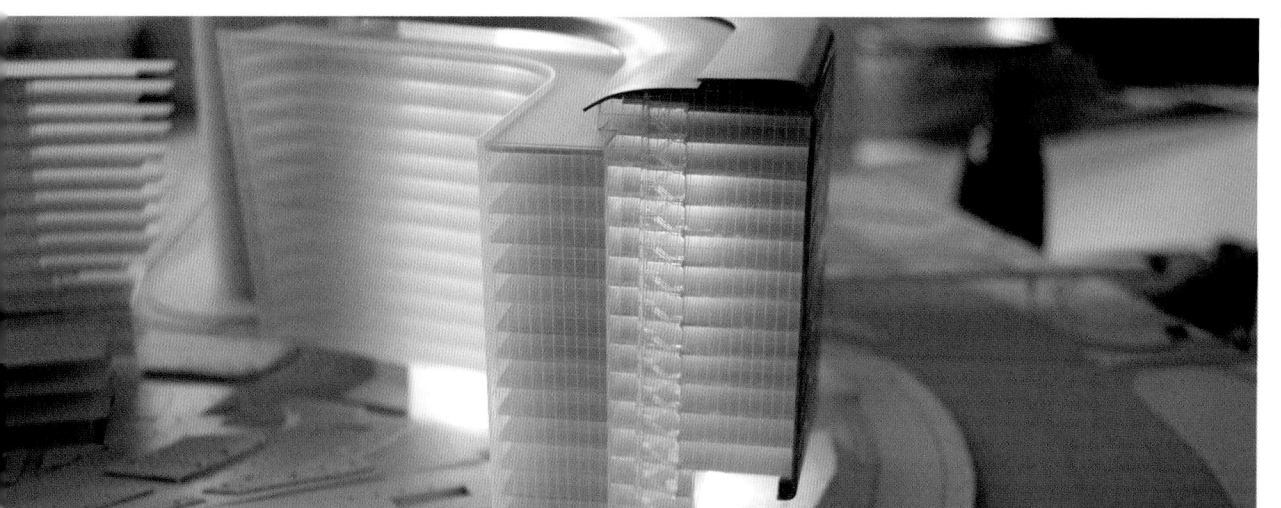

**Hong Kong Government
New Headquarters – Tamar**

Competition model
Dragages / Aedas 2007

1:500

By 2007, we had built models for many of the buildings along the Central and Wan Chai waterfront and had hoped this project would add to our list, but alas, this time our team did not win the competition.

Kai Tak Cruise Terminal Building

Hong Kong SAR
Dragages / Foster + Partners
1:500   2009

Sectional Model 1:50   6 Jul 2010

Dragages rang and asked me to fabricate their Cruise Terminal Building (CTB) competition model. I was working on my own at the time, so I turned down the job as the drawings would have arrived only a few days before the submission deadline and the pressure would have been too great.

A few weeks later, I was in Foster + Partners' office and Richard Hawkins told me they were designing the CTB for Dragages, and asked me to fabricate the working model during the design stage. A design/working model has to be simple and completed quickly, requiring good communication and understanding between the architects and model maker. Using the model, the design can then be changed or quickly modified.

The floor plate module was the first model completed. I made a two-module master and cast a silicone mould to duplicate modules when needed. When the setting out was ready, a base plate was made so the modules could be screwed onto it. I prefer screwing to gluing, as it is cleaner and easily reversed. The other designs — elevations, tail section, head section and roof — arrived from Foster's London office and after many design changes the design/working model took one and a half months to complete. Foster won the competition and I completed one further 1:50 sectional model for Foster + Partners to show the space and volume inside the CTB.

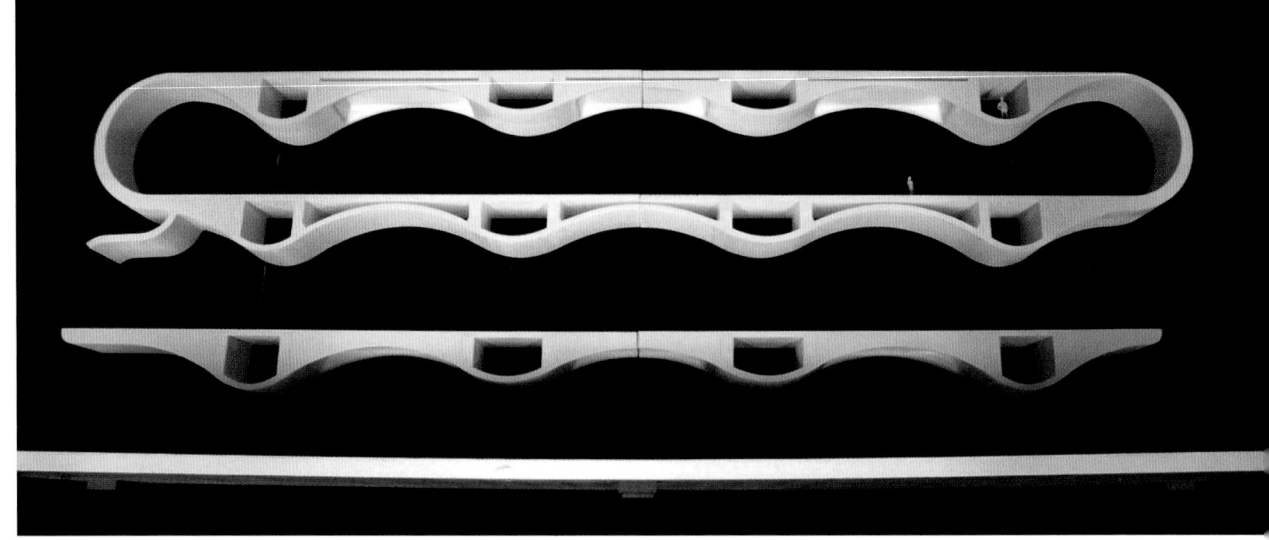

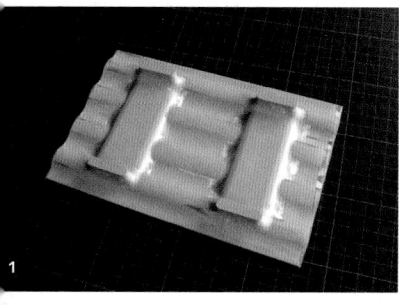

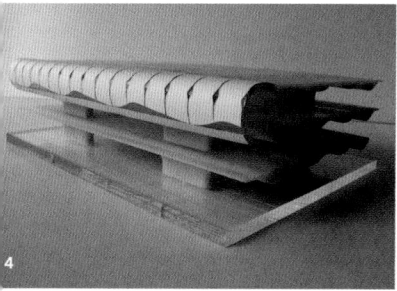

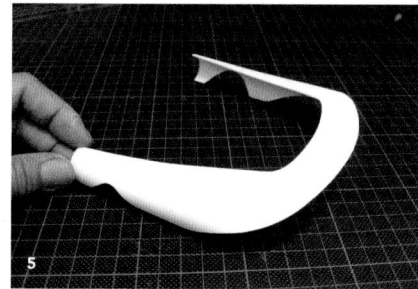

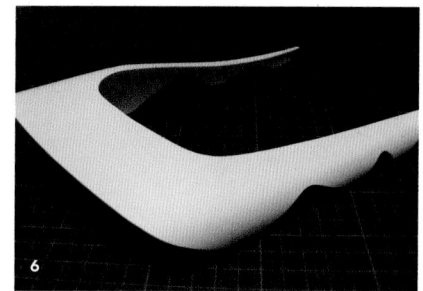

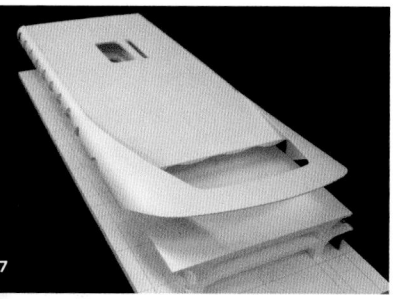

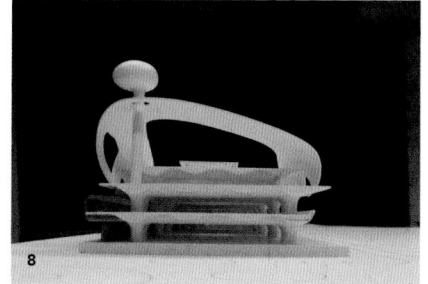

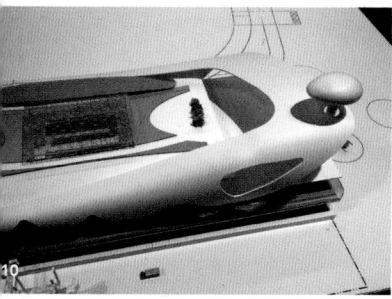

Working Models

1   Master for 2 typical bays 11 Sept 2009
2   Silicone mould for 2 typical bays 13 Sept 2009
3   Cast typical bays - 3 levels x 4 bays 18 Sept 2009
4   Seafront elevation 23 Sept 2009
5   Tail profile 27 Sept 2009
6   Head profile 30 Sept 2009
7   Tail section 2 Oct 2009
8   Head section 8 Oct 2009
9-11 Model completed 27 Oct 2009

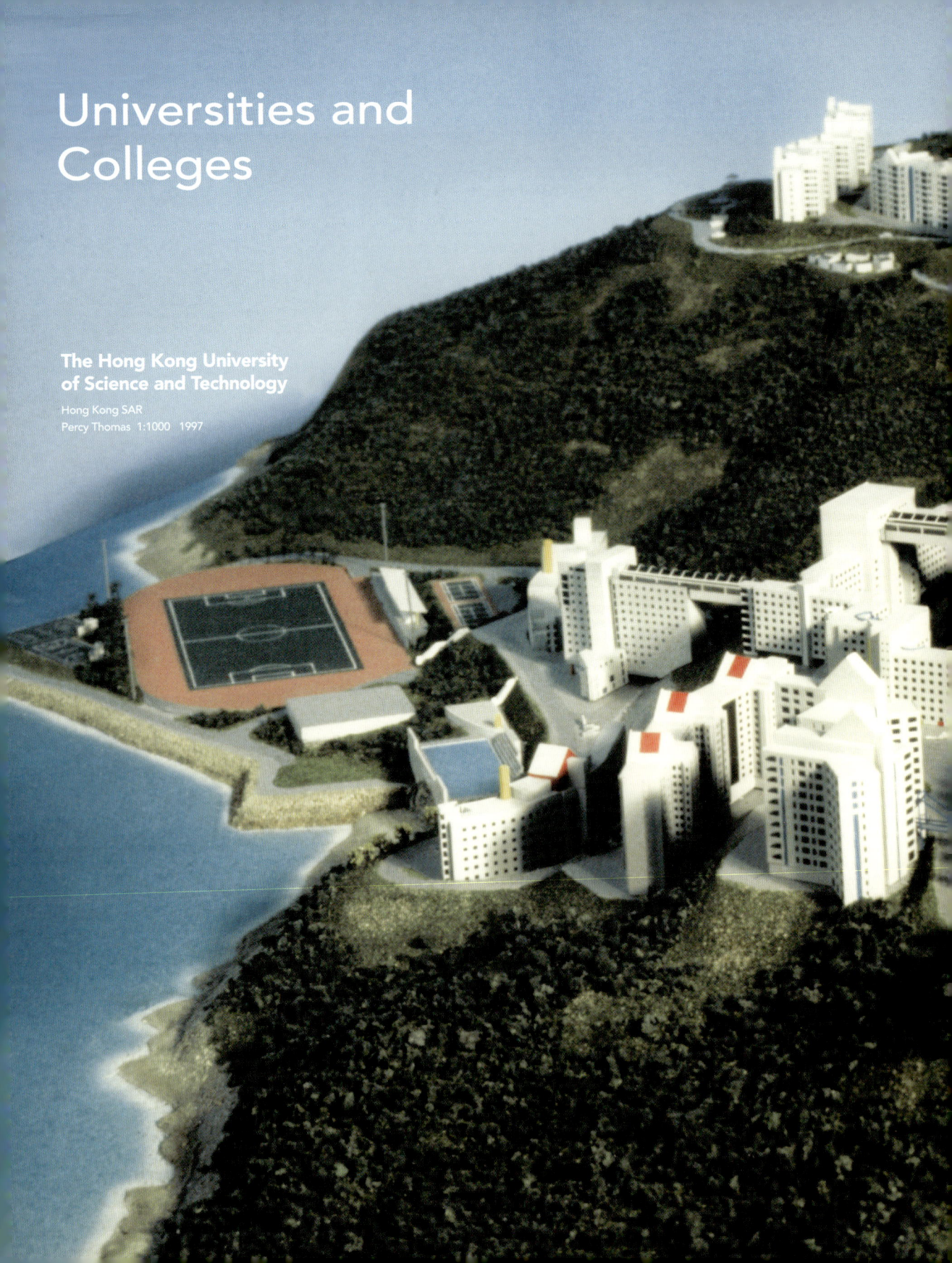

Universities and
Colleges

**The Hong Kong University
of Science and Technology**

Hong Kong SAR
Percy Thomas 1:1000 1997

The awarding of the design for The Hong Kong University of Science and Technology was controversial because the contract went to the runner-up, not the winner, of the design competition. Ten years later and completely out of the blue I was asked to build the model for the university's phase two development.

The Hong Kong University of Science and Technology

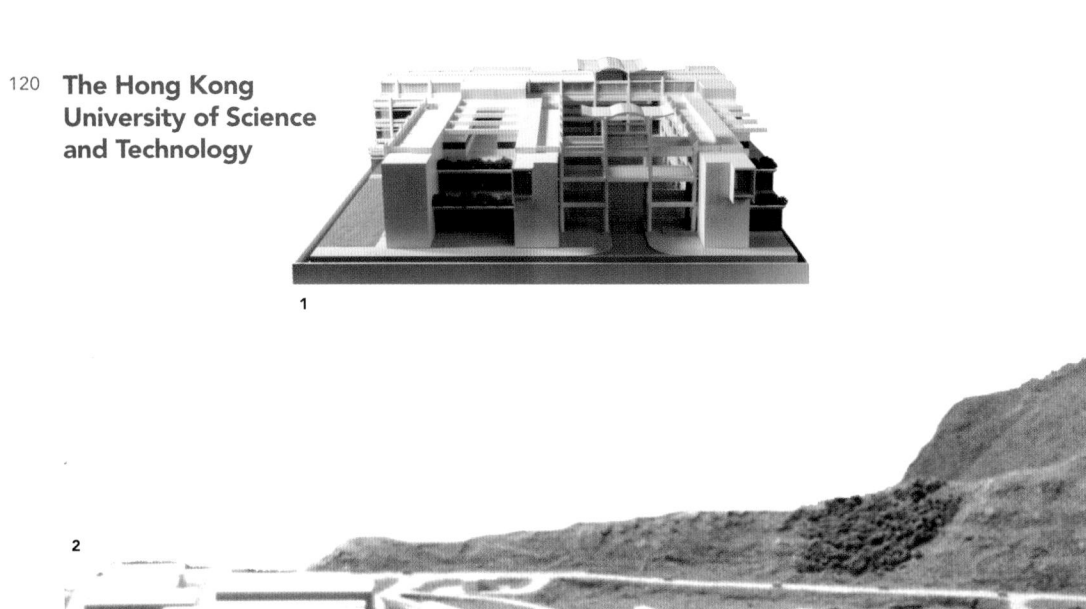

1

2

1:100 1987
Campus competition model
Hackett & Griffiths 1:500 1987

Located at Clear Water Bay with stunning views of the ocean, The Hong Kong University of Science and Technology offers a range of courses for undergraduate and postgraduate study and research opportunities.

Opportunities for university study have greatly increased over recent years as Hong Kong has evolved into a specialist logistics, financial and service-based economy requiring an educated workforce.

Study model Percy Thomas 1:100 1987

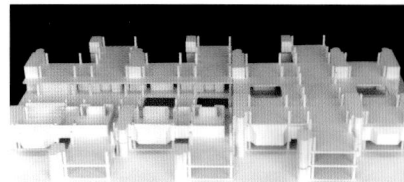

Planning model Percy Thomas 1:200 1986

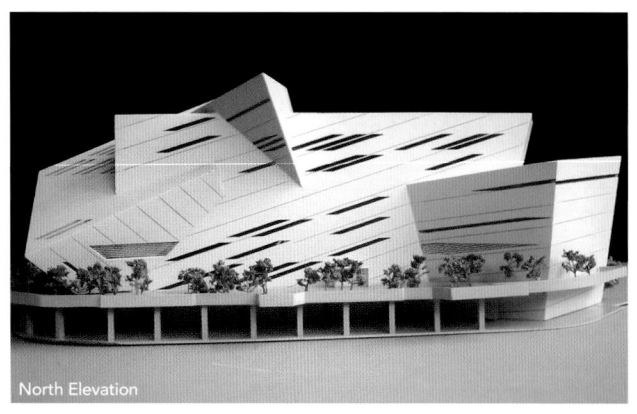

North Elevation

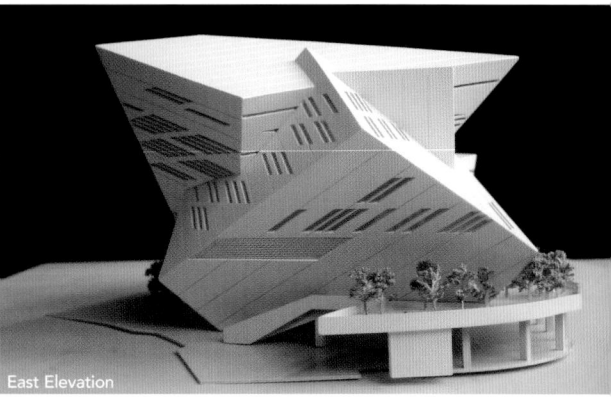

East Elevation

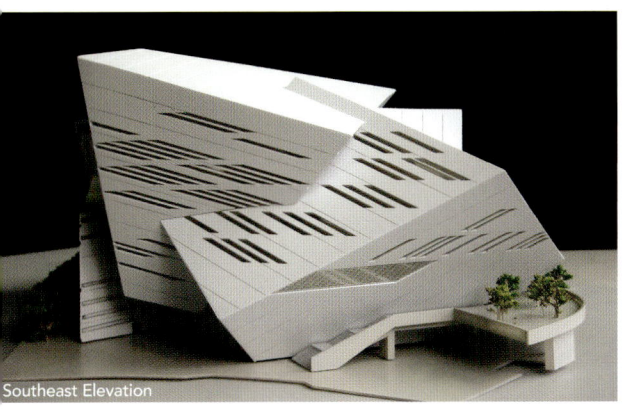

City University of
Hong Kong Campus

Hong Kong SAR
Percy Thomas 1:450 2000
updated 2005 / 2007

Southeast Elevation

South Elevation

City University of Hong Kong
School of Creative Media Building

Hong Kong SAR
Daniel Libeskind 1:450 2005

The Open University of Hong Kong

Hong Kong SAR
Percy Thomas 1:200 1994

The Open University of Hong Kong is one of many university institutions that have opened in the last twenty years. Our models of these institutions have similarly mapped Hong Kong's changing education landscape.

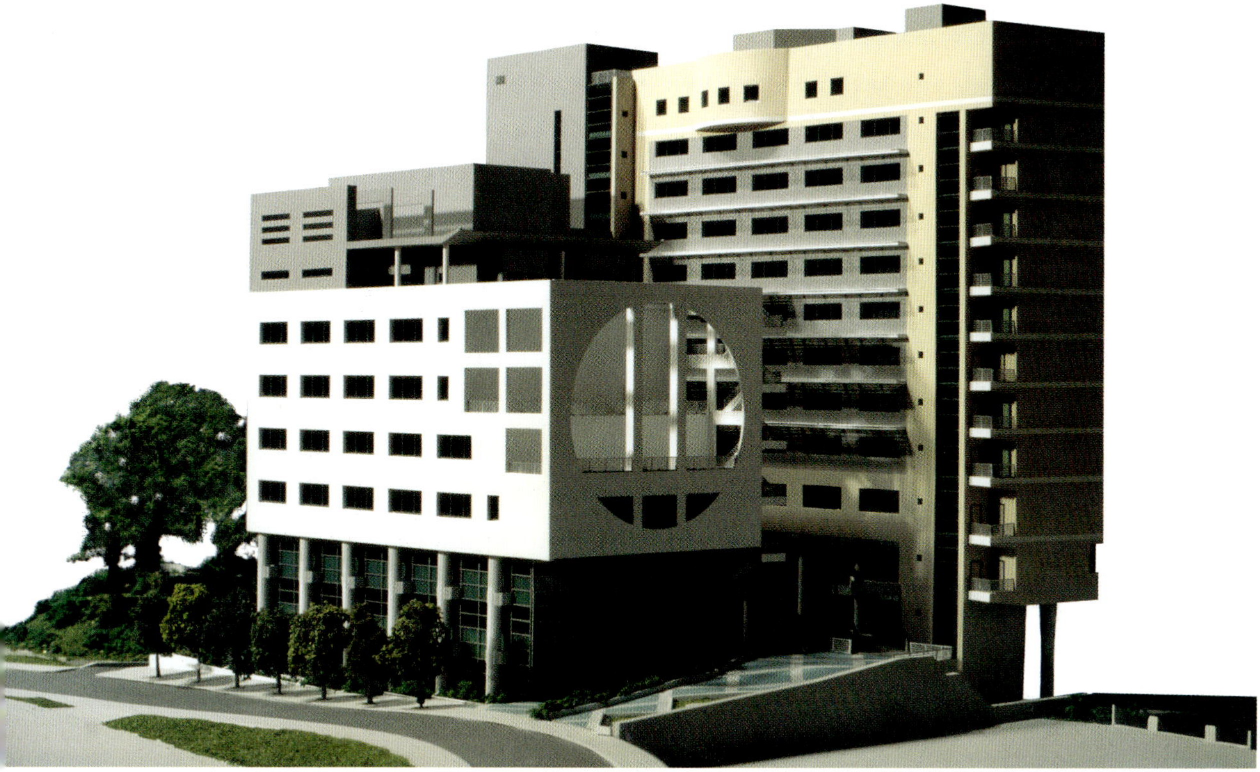

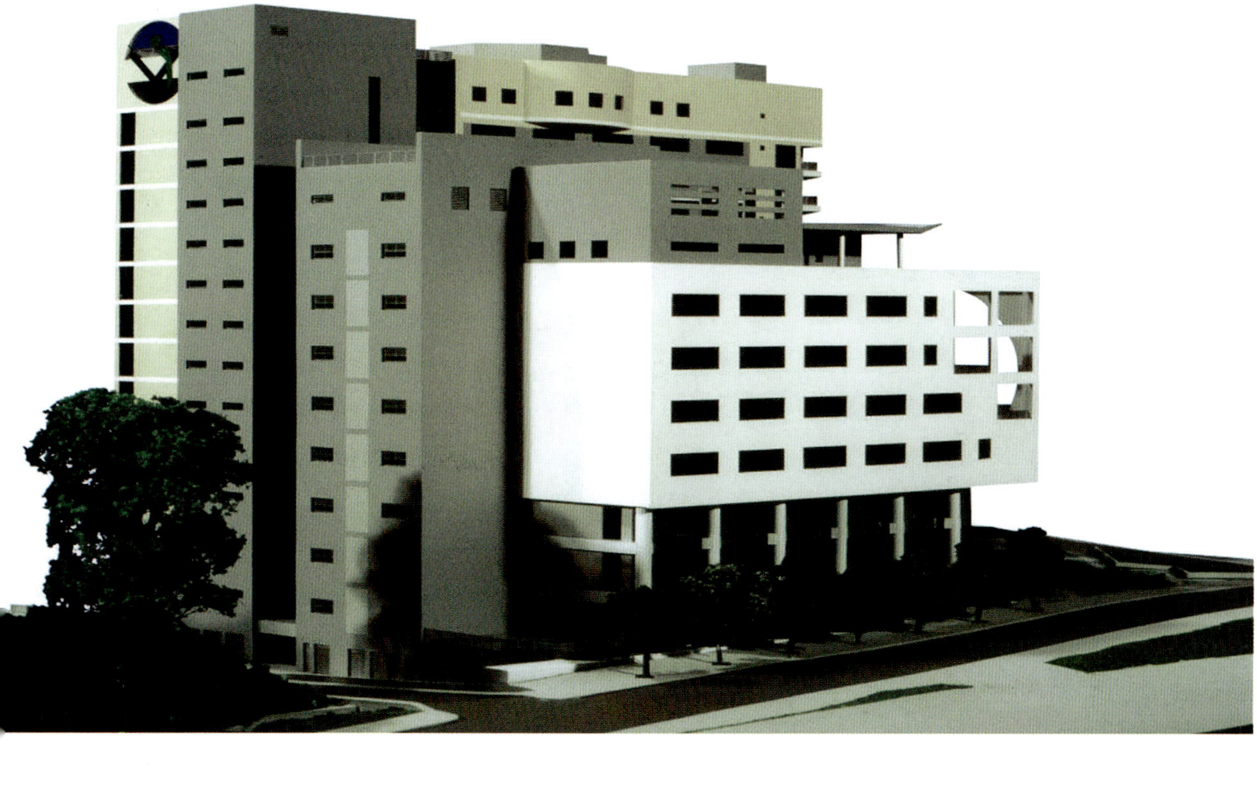

**Hong Kong
Baptist University**

Hong Kong SAR
Leigh & Orange 1999

1:300

St. Stephen's College

Science Laboratory
Hong Kong SAR
RMJM 1:150 2002

I studied for seven years as a boarder at St. Stephen's College in Stanley. Within its large and beautiful grounds, we had lots of free time between lessons, dinner and preparing our studies. During this free time I spent many happy hours making model airplanes, boats and cars – it was during those early school days that I first realised I liked to use my hands to make things.

In the 1961 summer holiday, Po, my brother and I built one of the very first kayaks in Hong Kong in the school carpentry workshop, all completed with our own hands. The kayak had a teak wood frame, covered with canvas and sealed with paint, and it took us the whole summer holiday to finish. We launched it together at St. Stephen's Beach and christened it for good luck with a bottle of Cream Soda. People gathered round and asked us where they could buy or get one – I proudly said we had built it ourselves! As I remember, our rowing club made a total of 4 - 6 kayaks, worthy of many rowing teams, and stored them in the St. Stephen's Old Boys' Association pavilion on the beach.

/inner of School
esign Competition

ng Kong SAR
1:200   2002

This is a generic design model. We used only four basic materials:
white acrylic for the buildings, clear acrylic for the glazing, olive
green foam for the landscape and natural maple for the base.

Museums

博物館

Chinese Village

National Museum of Natural Science
Taichung, Taiwan
1:30   1992

Chinese Village

National Museum of Natural Science
Taichung, Taiwan
1:30   1992

This is the best landscape model we ever built. It is so realistic that even I find it hard to believe these are photographs of a model. If you look carefully, you can see farmers doing their chores and fetching water from a well under the midday sun; pigs and their piglets snoozing and searching for roots to eat; ducks pecking for food around the muddy banks of the pond; and, dogs wandering aimlessly and guarding the village. One can actually feel the peace, quietness and tranquility of village life.

The materials used in this model are mostly natural: soil was dug from a rice paddy field, sieved and mixed with white glue. The building's roof and dry hay were made of coconut husk; and, grass and scrub were real plants picked from the wild.

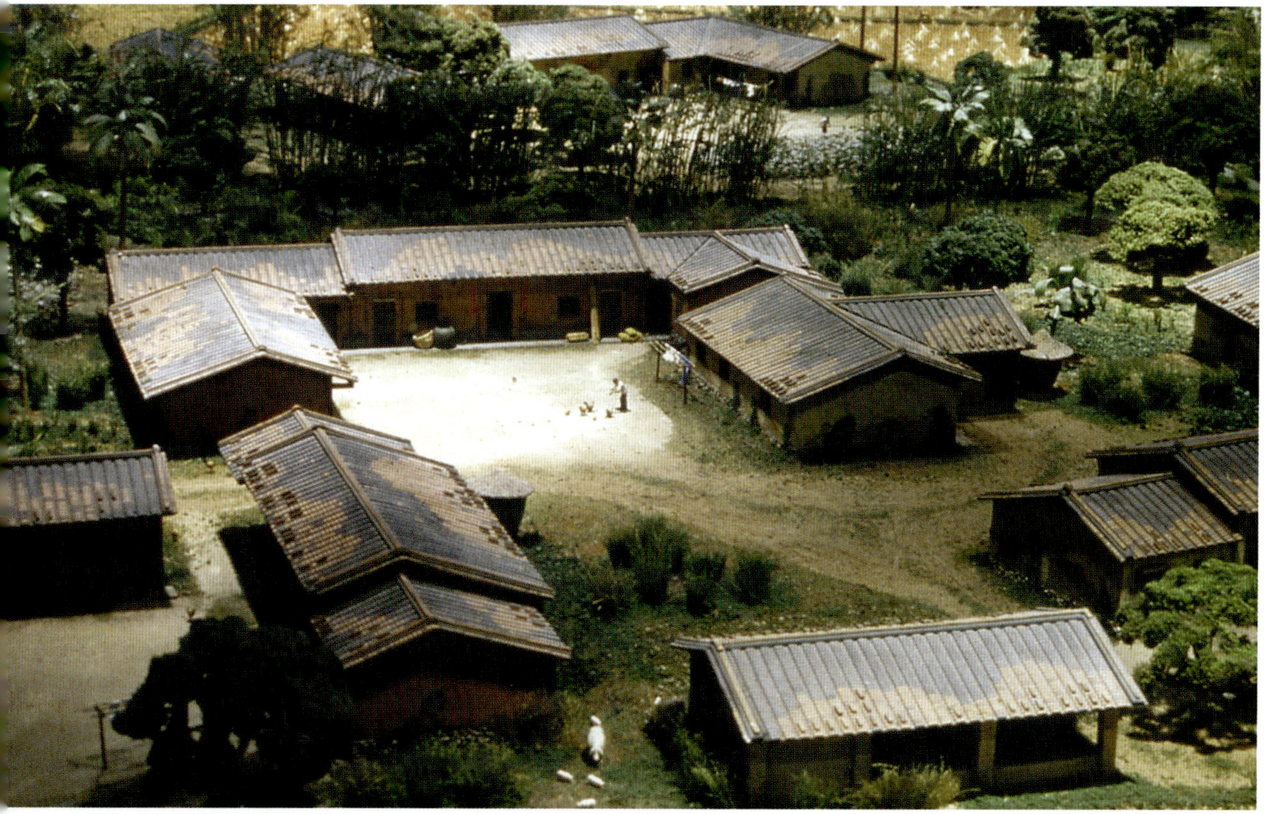

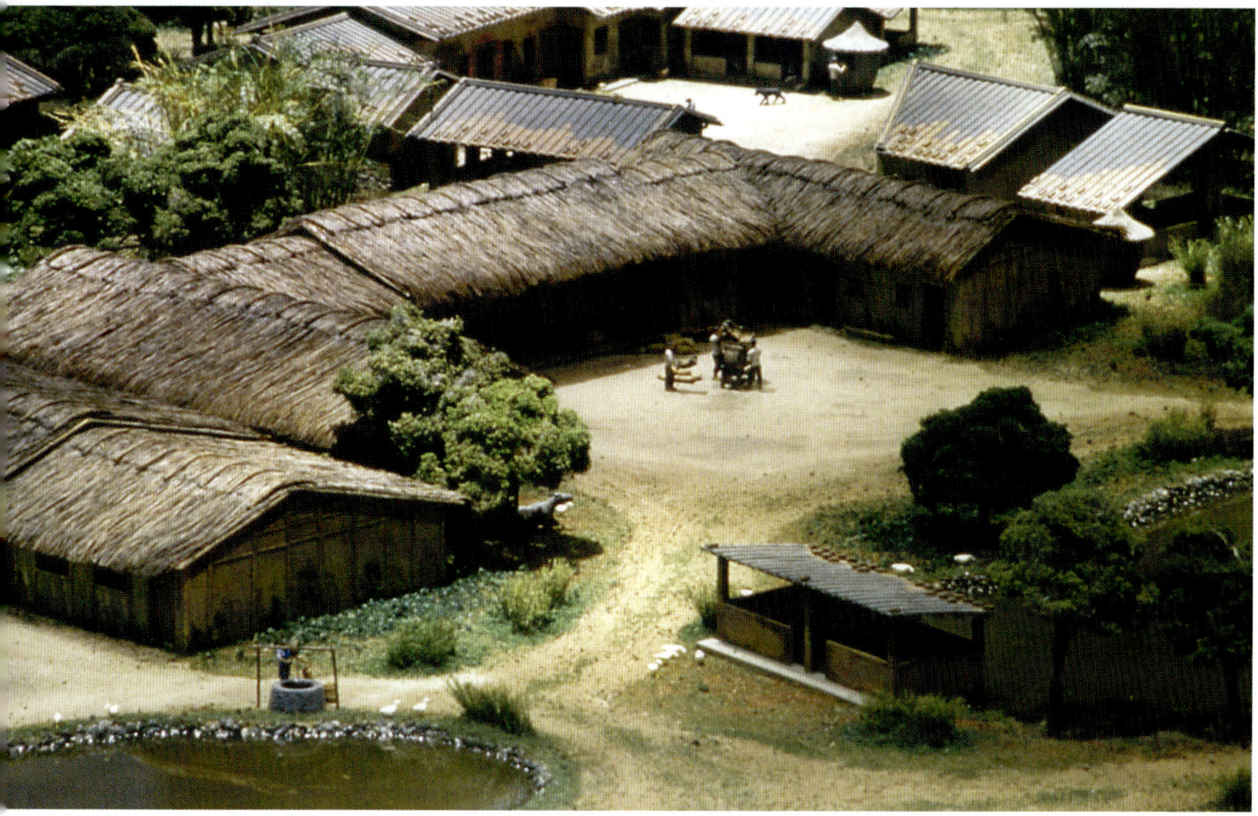

National Palace Museum

National Palace Museum
Taipei, Taiwan
1:200   1994

Details of National Palace Museum 1994

1:200

Kowloon-Canton Railway Station

Hong Kong SAR
Hong Kong Railway Museum
1:87

This model was built in 1992 after the Kowloon-Canton Railway Station was demolished in 1978. Only the original clock tower, built in 1921, is still standing on the actual site. We sourced many old photographs to help us build this model.
The Kowloon-Canton Railway Station was the starting point of the long overland railway journey connecting Hong Kong to Europe, via Beijing, the Trans-Siberian Railway across Russia to Moscow and then onwards for connections to all European destinations.

Tu Lou

Hong Kong SAR
Leisure and Cultural Services Department
1:100

Village School

Hong Kong SAR
Sam Tung Uk Museum
1:50   1996

Dragon Bone Waterwheel

Hong Kong SAR
Sam Tung Uk Museum
5   1991

This model was made entirely of wood and the paddles of the waterwheel can actually push water up to the trough.

Canton Factories

Hong Kong SAR
Hong Kong Museum of Art
1:35 1990

We were given a copy of the
painting below to recreate a model
of the foreign 'factories' located
on the Pearl River in 19th century
Canton (Guangzhou).

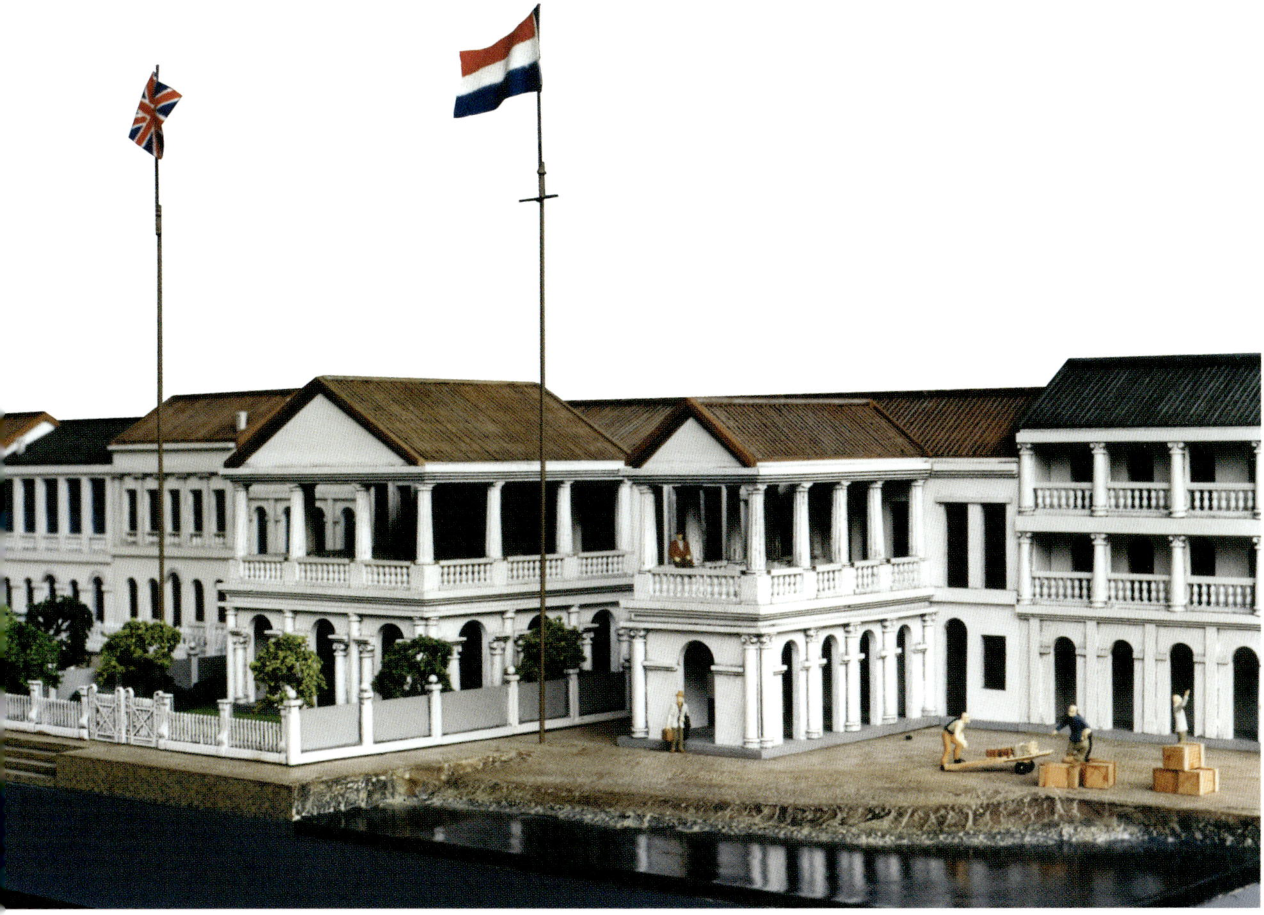

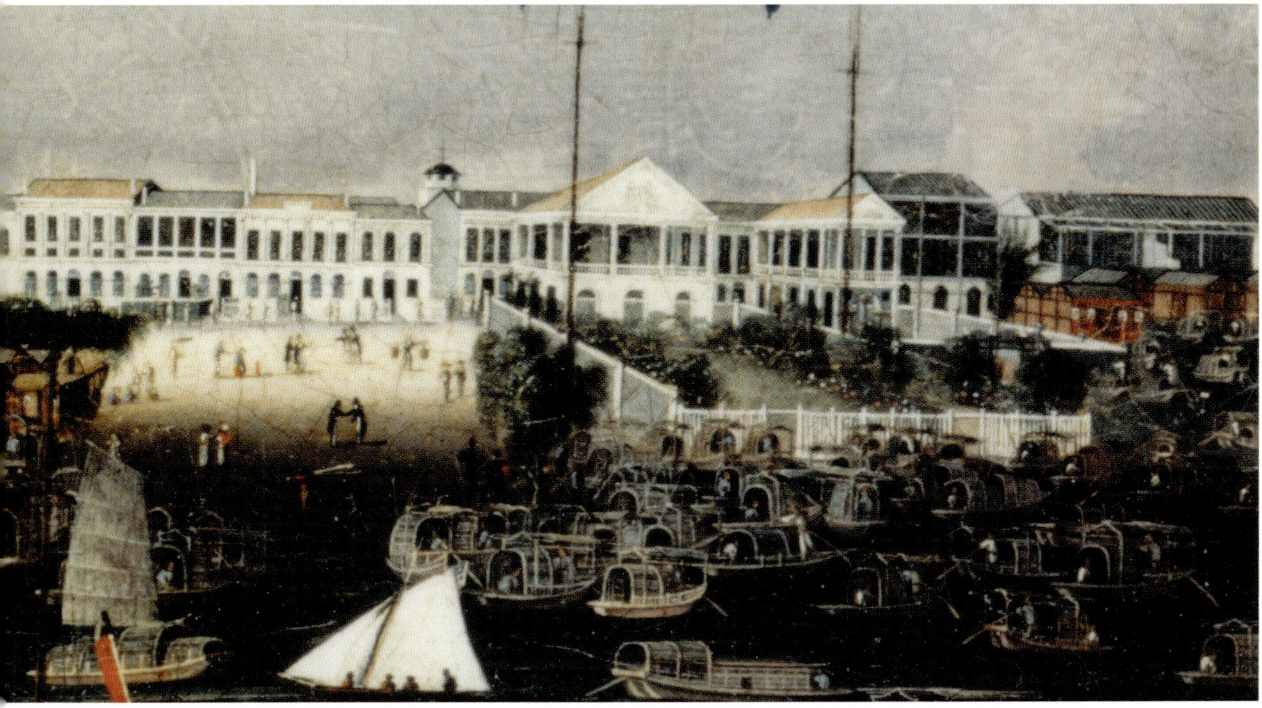

Landscapes

A landscape setting can bring a model to life — it can make or break a model.
We can recreate a landscape by using different materials in innovative ways. For example, we beat foam in a food blender and then colour the pieces into different shades of green and brown. Once we have these basic materials, we can then make different sized trees, scrub, grass or anything we might need. We usually use two basic colour schemes for landscapes, realistic and pastel. Realistic landscapes are usually done for finished models while a pastel colour scheme is used for concept models requiring a subdued background.

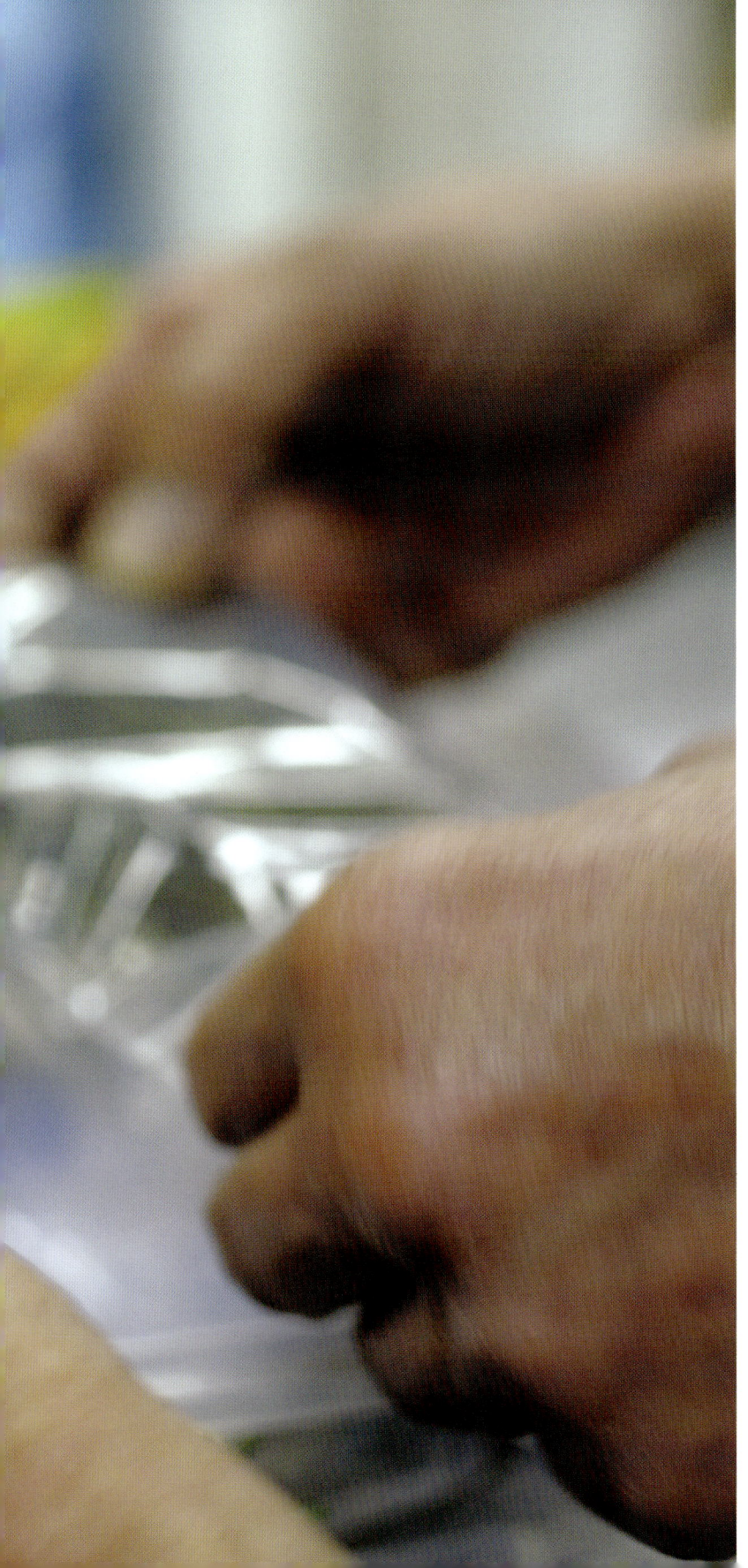

Natural material landscapes
1:90

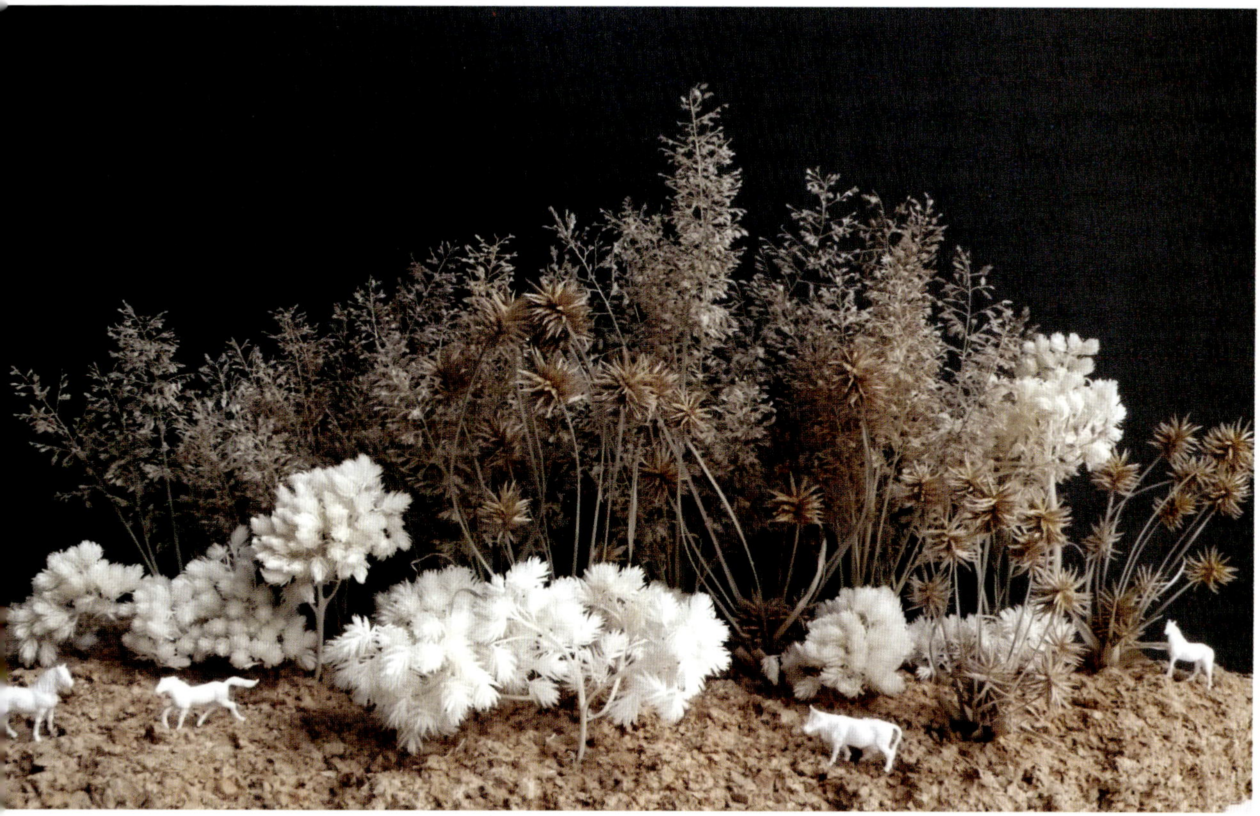

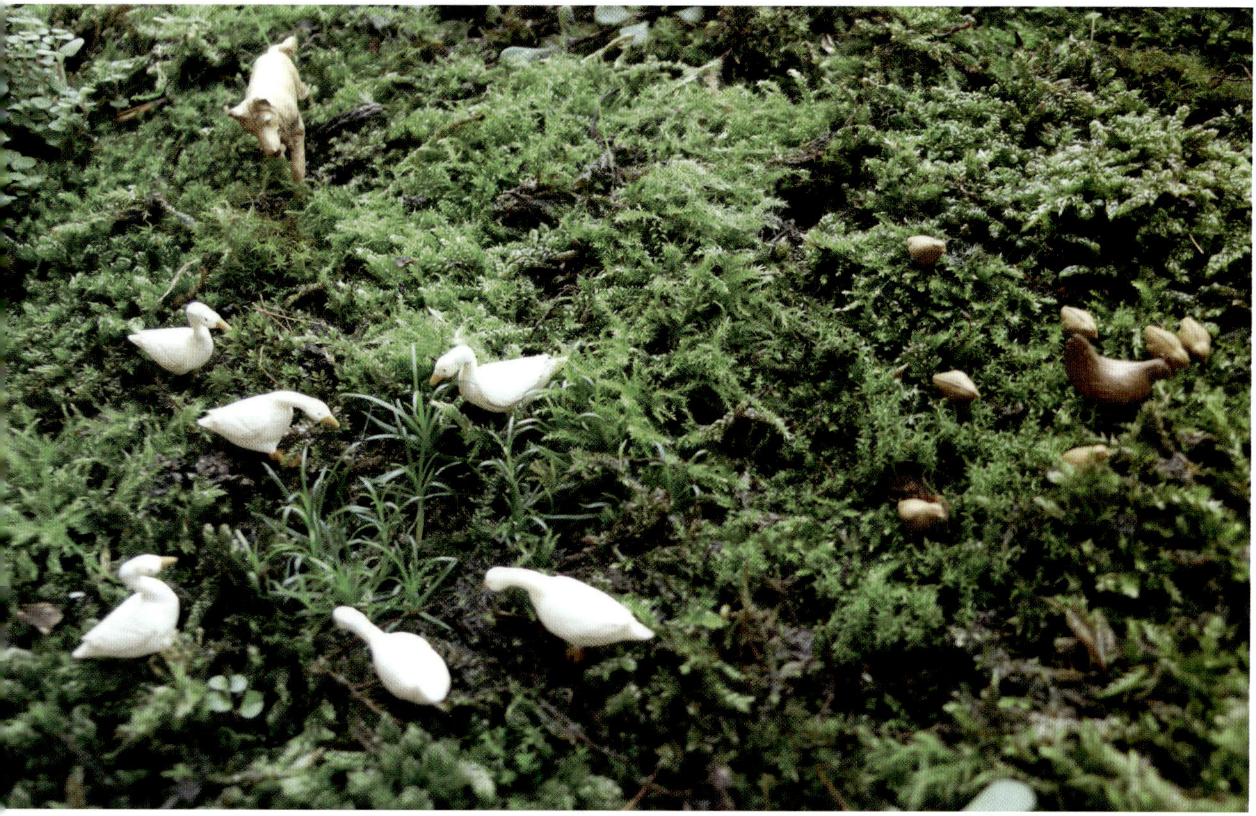

Cyberport

Hong Kong SAR
PCCW
Urbis 1:200 2002

Commercial
Buildings

Central, Hong Kong

Hong Kong SAR
Hongkong Land 1:500
updated 2001

Buildings for which we have made models dot the entire Hong Kong landscape and visitors arriving from China by train will see many of them as they travel around the city until they finally make their way to Hong Kong International Airport and fly to other places in the world.

商廈

Chater House

Hong Kong SAR
Hongkong Land
KPF / LPT 1:200   2001

York House

The Landmark Mandarin Oriental Hotel
Hong Kong SAR
Hongkong Land
PF / LPT 1:300 2002

A sample journey passing some of the buildings for which we have fabricated models:

Arrive at Lo Wo Station > East Rail Line > East Tsim Sha Tsui Station > Tsim Sha Tsui Station Interchange > MTR > Central Station > The Landmark > Coffee in The Landmark Mandarin Oriental Hotel > Withdraw cash from the Standard Chartered Bank or HSBC > Footbridges around Central Hong Kong > Prince's Building > Alexandra House > Shop for luxury world brands > Chater House > Stay a night at the Four Seasons Hotel > See your financial adviser at IFC I > Buy a BoBo from Qeelin at IFC II > Check in at Hong Kong Station > Airport Express > Travel over the Tsing Ma Bridge > Ground Transport Centre > Shop at Sky Plaza > Go through Immigration at the Hong Kong International Airport.

Alexandra House

Hong Kong SAR
Hongkong Land
LPT 1:100 2001
Exploded marketing model for
expansion and renovation

Standard Chartered Bank

Hong Kong SAR
P&T 1:400 1985

The renovation and upgrading of Hongkong Land's core shopping arcades set the trend for luxury designer brands opening their flagship stores in Central. The city's free-port status and absence of sales taxes has enabled Hong Kong to continue its reputation as a shopping destination.

The Landmark and neighbouring bank buildings

Hong Kong SAR
Hongkong Land
2 Standard Chartered Bank P&T 1:400 1985
3 The Landmark renovation LPT 1:300 2001
4 The Landmark new façade KPF 2003

Entertainment Building

Hong Kong SAR
Chinese Estates
Hackett & Griffiths 1:150 1987

his was the first model for which we
ed in-house brass photo-etching
 the façade of the building.

Details of brass photo-etching, actual model size

The Entertainment Building was
previously known as King's Theatre.
This model was built before it was
demolished to make way for its
redevelopment.

International Finance Centre II

IFC I / IFC II / Airport Express Hong Kong Station/
Four Seasons Hotel
Hong Kong SAR
Central Waterfront
Caesar Pelli / Rocco Design / Draughtzman
2001

1:200

A meeting called by the architects of International Finance Centre II and attended by most of the large model making companies in Hong Kong outlined three large modelling jobs open for tender — namely, IFC II; the Podium with the Airport Express and Hong Kong Station; and, the Centrepiece Full Site. The deadline for completion of all the models was two months. I considered that IFC II would be an iconic building for many years to come and for a project of such importance and magnitude:

1 The architects would want a high quality model.
2 With many parties involved and so much money at stake, no mistakes would be accepted.

I thought, if we could not complete the models within this timeframe, then probably no other model maker could either (this was prior to the opening of large model making shops in Shenzhen). I took a big gamble and declined to submit a quotation because the schedule was too tight. A few days later, the Centrepiece Full Site model was placed for bid again with the deadline extended to three months. The Tower and Podium jobs had been allocated. There were two ways of viewing the situation: negatively, because we had no work, or positively, as having no work, we were now able to bid on this job. We did bid and got the job.

We put all the resources of our seven model makers into the job. I was responsible for brass photo-etching/nickel plating and the Four Seasons Hotel section. My colleagues took the following sections: Mike was responsible for the base, site, roads and covered walkways. Raymond and Pang worked on the IFC II Tower; Wing took up the IFC I Tower; and, Fung and Brian were responsible for the Podium. The complete model was finished within two and a half months, and was the centrepiece of the IFC I show suite overlooking Victoria Harbour and the IFC II site.

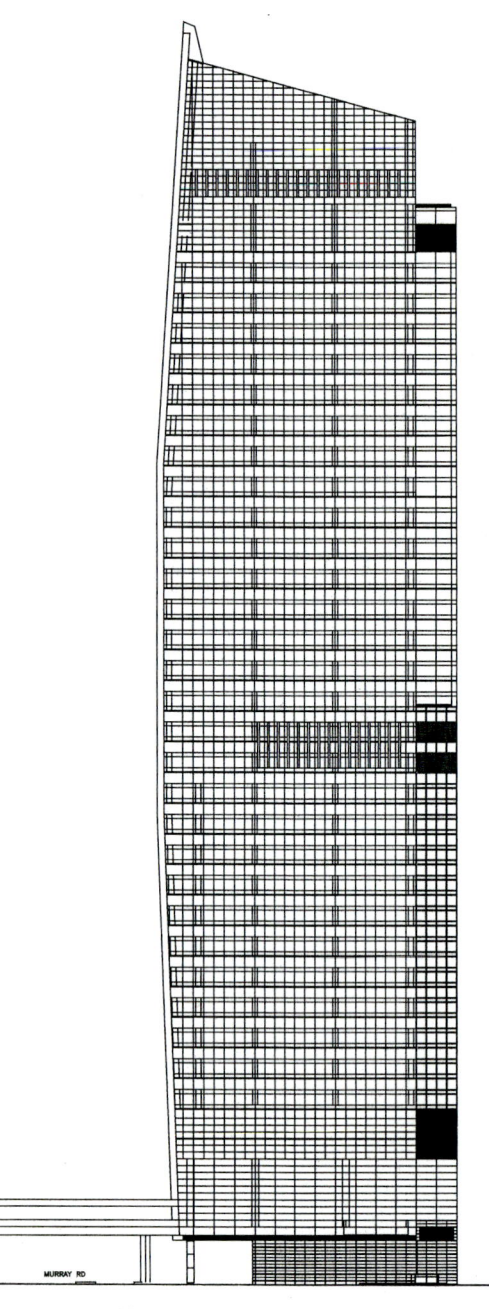

Image produced from laser-cutting file

This was the first 1:200 model in which we incorporated a ceiling light effe

AIG

Hong Kong SAR
Capital Land
SOM / LPT 1:200 2002

1 Model night scene
3 Actual building at night

Peak Tower
Peak Tram Terminus

Competition model
Hong Kong SAR
Hong Kong & Shanghai Hotels
Hackett Design 1:200   1991

**Beijing China
Resources Building**

Beijing, PRC
HOK 1:250 1996

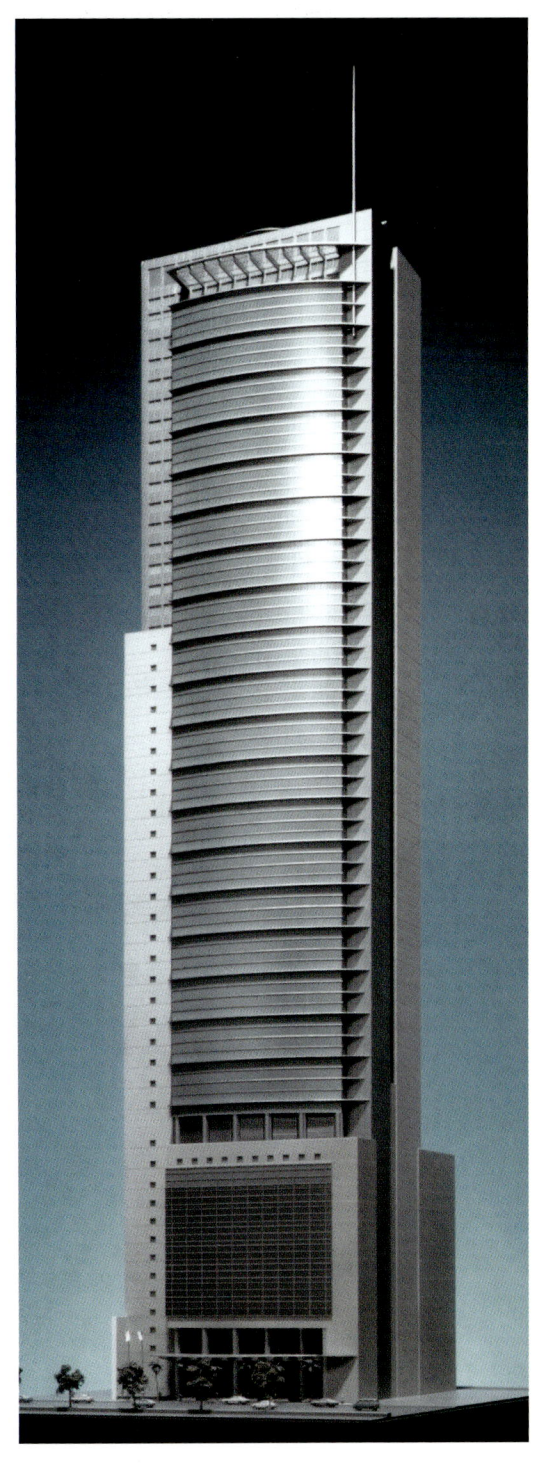

Jaka Tower

Manila, The Philippines
HOK 1:150 1995

South Pacific Plaza

Shanghai, PRC
HOK 1:200 1996

China Merchants
International Finance Centre

Beijing, PRC
China Merchants Bank
HOK 1:300 1995

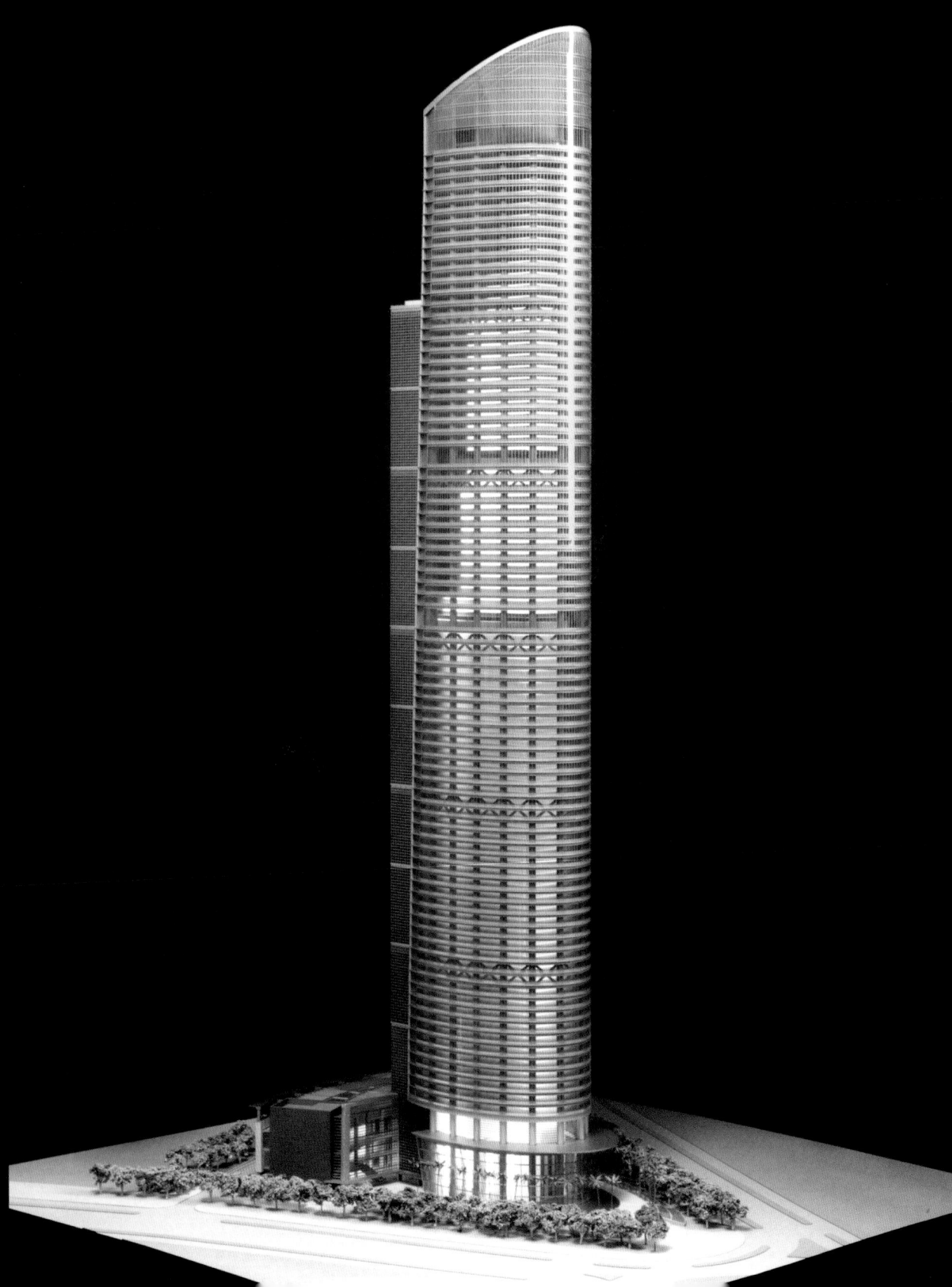

Fairwell Tower

Xiamen, PRC
HOK 1:300 1998

Jakarta, Indonesia
ArcPac 1:200 1990

Menara Kencana

Jakarta, Indonesia
ArcPac 1:200 1997

Allied Plaza

Hong Kong SAR
Allied Property
TAOHO Design 1:90 1987

South China Morning Post

Hong Kong SAR
TB 1:100 1993

Wong Chuk Hang Substation

Hong Kong Electric
Hong Kong SAR
200 2001

Plaza Indonesia in Jakarta, Indonesia was our first overseas model project and also the first model we built for HOK. We built 4 models in 2 different colours to help the Plaza Indonesia owners decide which colour to use for this building. Subsequently, we worked on many more projects for HOK and on countless overseas model projects for a variety of architectural firms.

Plaza Indonesia

Jakarta, Indonesia
HOK 1:200 1985

Grand Hotel

Kuala Lumpur, Malaysia
HOK 1:200 1990

Pacific Place II

Sukhumvit Road, Bangkok, Thailand
First Pacific Land & Partners
Hackett & Griffiths 1:200 1989

Pacific Plaza

Scotts Road, Singapore
LPT 1:200 1990

Pacific Mall

Johor Bahru, Malaysia
LET Pacific
LPT 1:200 1993

Twin Tower

Tao & Kinoshita 1:200 1991

un Razak I

ala Lumpur, Malaysia
OK 1:150 1996

Tun Razak II

Kuala Lumpur, Malaysia
HOK 1:150 1997

Cameron Centre

Hong Kong SAR
Yuncken Freeman 1:200 1988

aigon Centre

Chi Minh City, Vietnam
CM 1:400 1992

Saigon Centre

Ho Chi Minh City, Vietnam
DCM 1:200 1994

Guangzhou Daily

Guangzhou, PRC
Terry Farrell 1:300 1999

Residential Buildings

G House

Shanghai, PRC
Peter Fung 1:150 1994

A few weeks after we delivered the model for the
`G House´, I received a call from Peter Fung's secretary
saying they were having the launch party for the
property that night and the model's lights would not
turn on, "Could you come to Gaddi's straight away?"
I asked where Gaddi's was. She gasped, "What do
you mean, everybody knows where Gaddi's is. It is in
the Peninsula Hotel!" So, I grabbed my tool bag and
rushed over.
The hotel's doorman stopped me and politely said, "Sir,
you are not dressed for the occasion." I was in my usual
T-shirt and jeans. I told him I only came to fix the model
and could he tell the host I had arrived. Peter came out
and said everything was working fine - they had just
forgotten to push the timer button! Then I suddenly
realised why people wear tuxedos with jeans!

住宅

**Carmen's Garden
9 Cox's Road**

Hong Kong SAR
Eton
RMJM 1996

1:150

We tried never to undertake residential model projects that had
many towers because we did not want to spend lots of time
assembling bay windows and air conditioners! This model was,
however, an exception as we were the only model maker that
RMJM employed and so we could not refuse the job.
We did not have a laser-cutter at the time, so we sent the files
to the United States to have all the parts laser cut. On their
return we sprayed and assembled the model in Hong Kong. This
project showed us the potential of AutoCAD and laser cutting.

Hong Kong SAR
Aedas
2007

1:300

Daiichi

Manila, The Philippines
HOK 1:200 1997

Freshwater Place

Sydney, Australia
Australand
Bates Smart 1:200 2003

One Mckinley Place

Manila, The Philippines
HOK 1:250 1997

Two Mckinley Place

Manila, The Philippines
HOK 1:250 2004

Phuket, Thailand
BRATIC PCMH 1:50 2001

Vancouver, Canada
1:75 1990

Caribbean Coast

Hong Kong SAR
Cheung Kong
Hsin Yieh 2000

185

RESIDENTIAL BUILDINGS

1:150

I like wood for its warmth, colour and texture. However, in Asia wood is not often used as a modelling medium because it is not considered to be sufficiently high-tech.

Dubai Opera House

Aedas 1:2000 2006

Andrew Bromberg gave me a photocopy of a glass sculpture, wanting the
Dubai Opera House model to have the same feel. He wished the model to
be finely elegant but with a rough edge. I had one week. So, I chose brass,
resin and walnut to give the desired visual impression.

The Legs

Aedas 2005

1:750

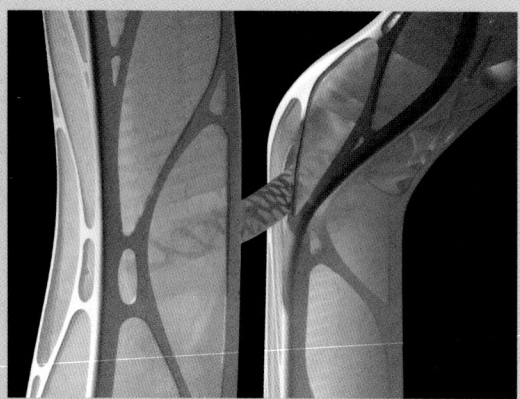

Model after glazing

It is easy to make a bad model out of a good design. It is difficult to make a good model out of a bad design. 'The Legs' is a good model, but was difficult to make from the 'far-out' design that had been provided to us. There were no true elevations. There was not one continuous vertical straight line from the base to the top of the building. There was no join line on the external structure. Where should we start? The only place to start, of course for a model maker: the lift core.

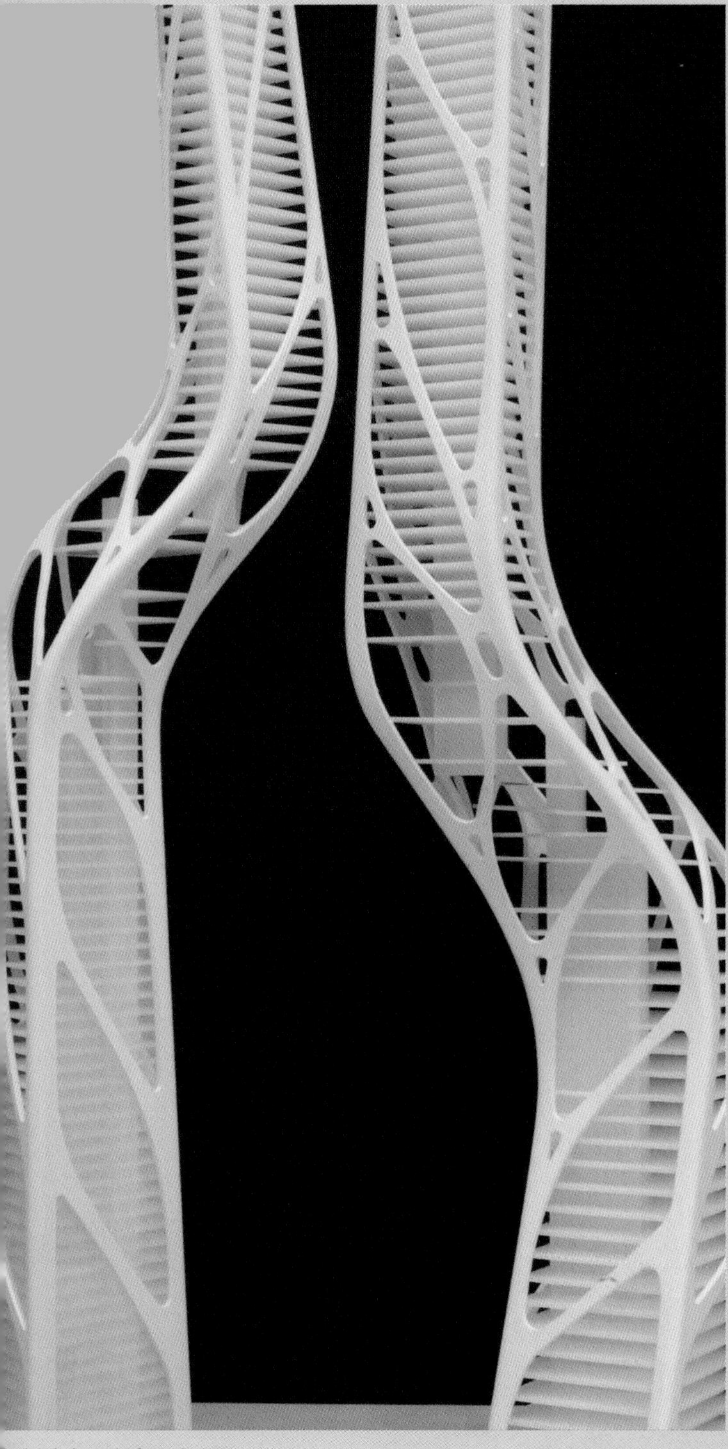

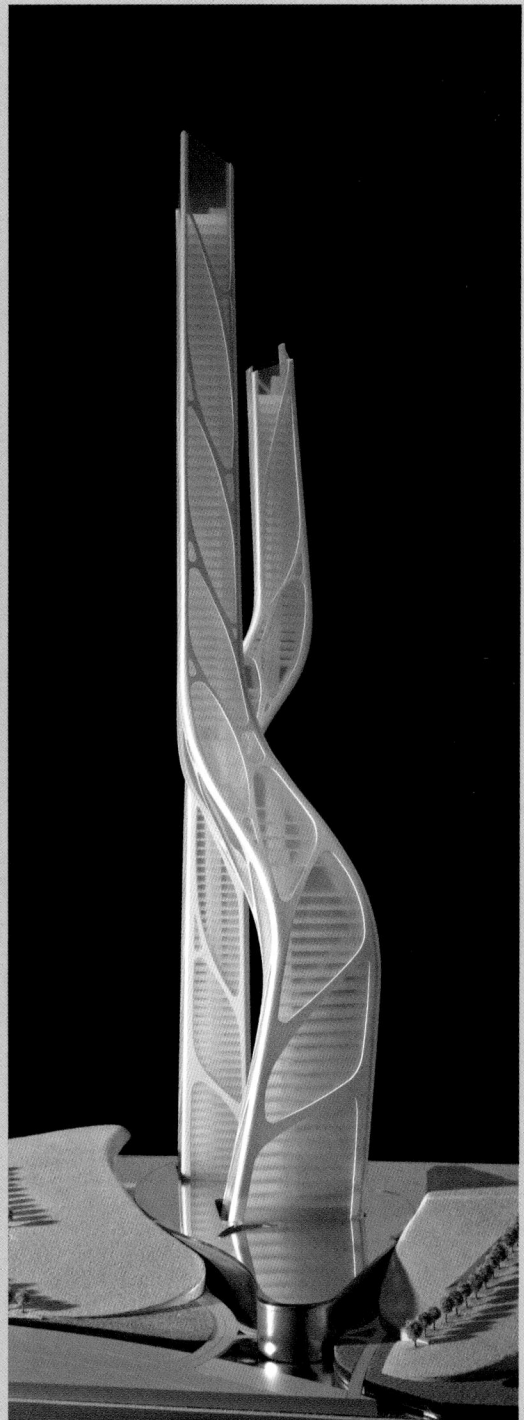

Model skeleton before glazing
500   2006

Dubai Media Tower

Aedas 1:750 2006

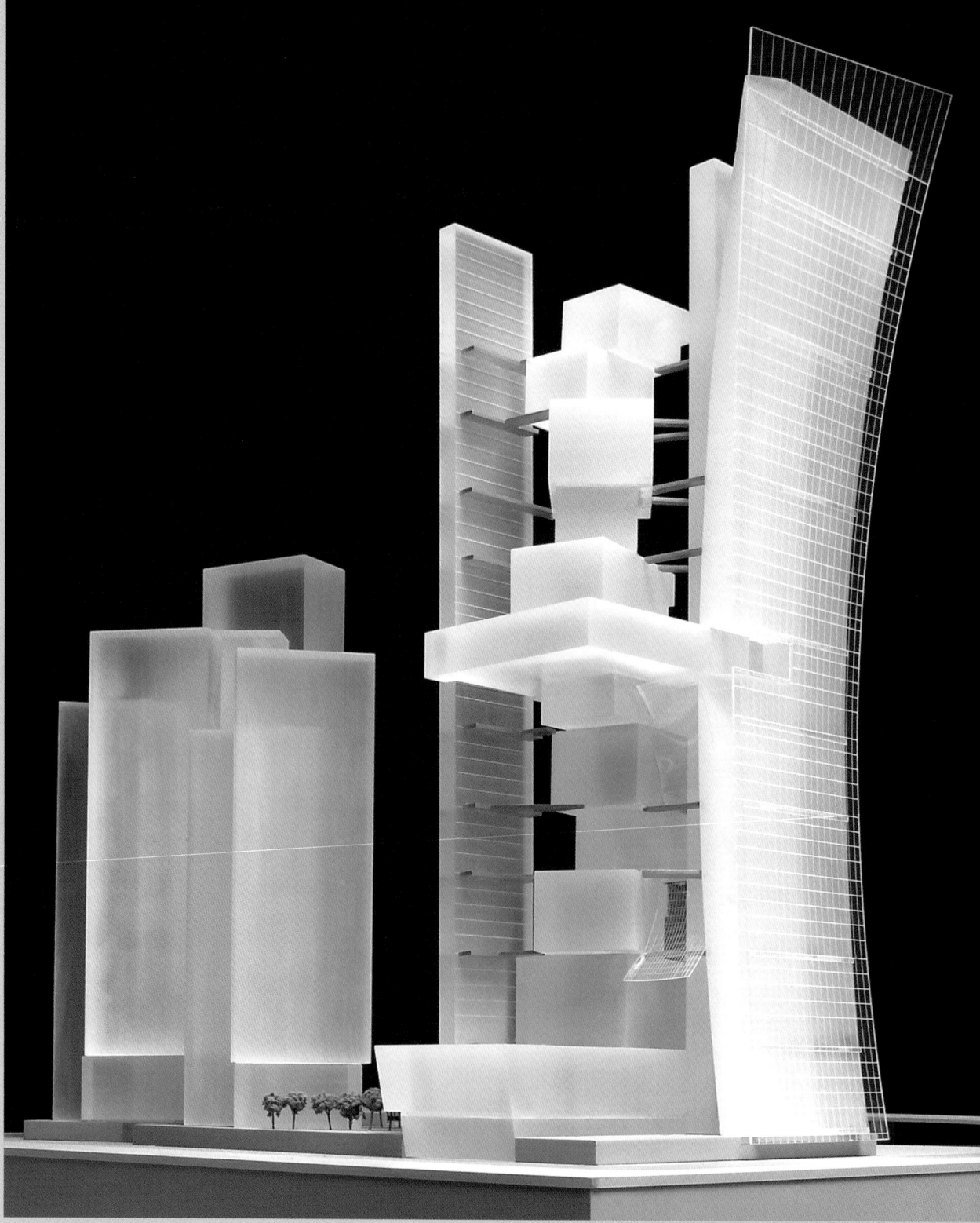

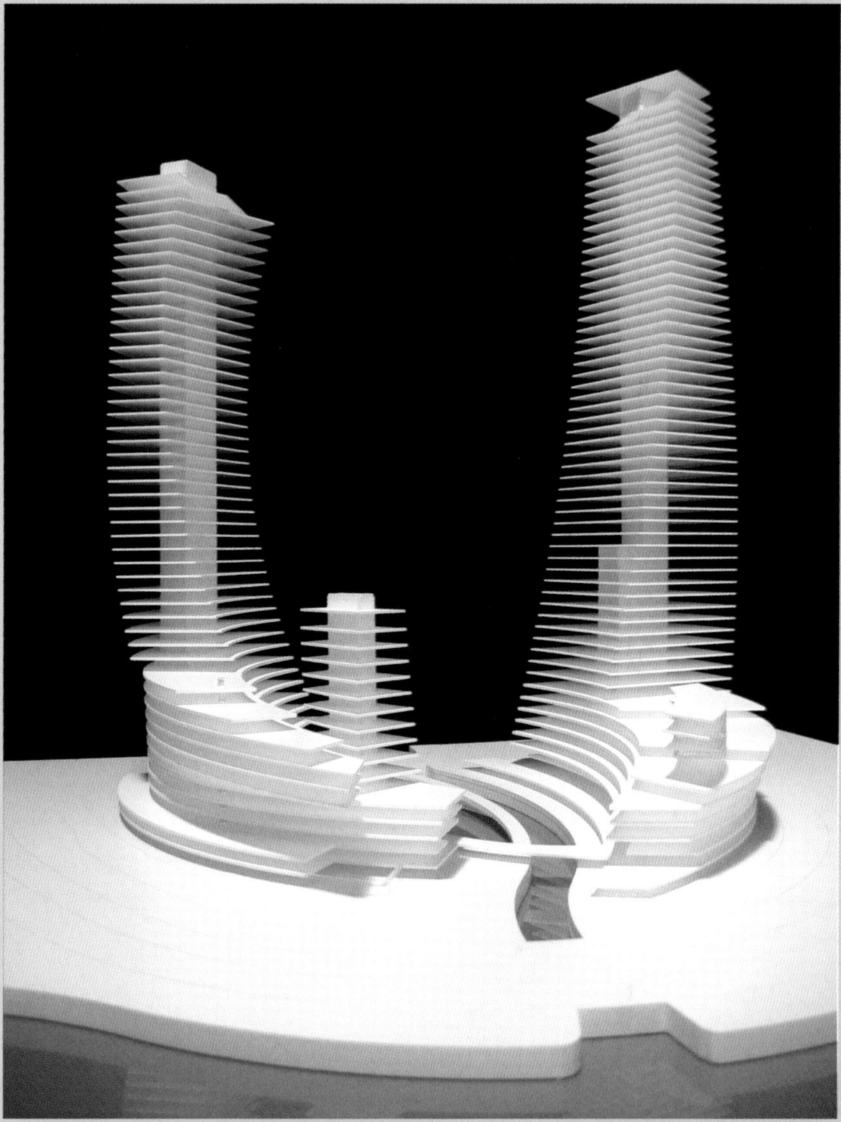

oroush Master Plan

ou Dhabi
edas 2005

:500

azhou Office Hotel Complex

uangzhou, PRC
m Fung
edas 2007

1:1000

DongZhiMen mixed-use development

Beijing, PRC
Aedas 2005

1:300

Zhonghuan International Plaza

Beijing, PRC
Aedas 1:1000 2003

Emaar Tower

Dubai
Aedas 1:750 2005

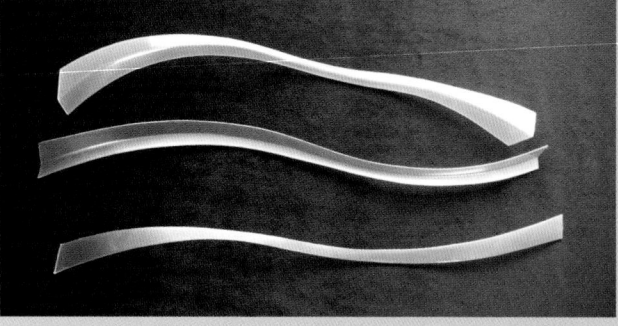

Hong Kong Express Rail Link

Hong Kong SAR
West Kowloon Terminus
Roof profile study models
Aedas 1:500 2008

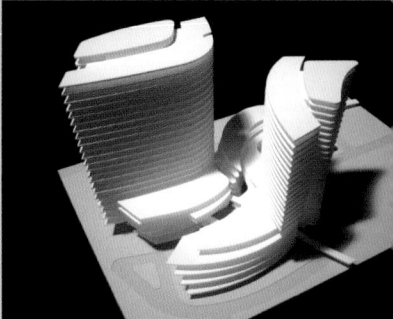

North Star

PRC
Aedas 1:500 2004

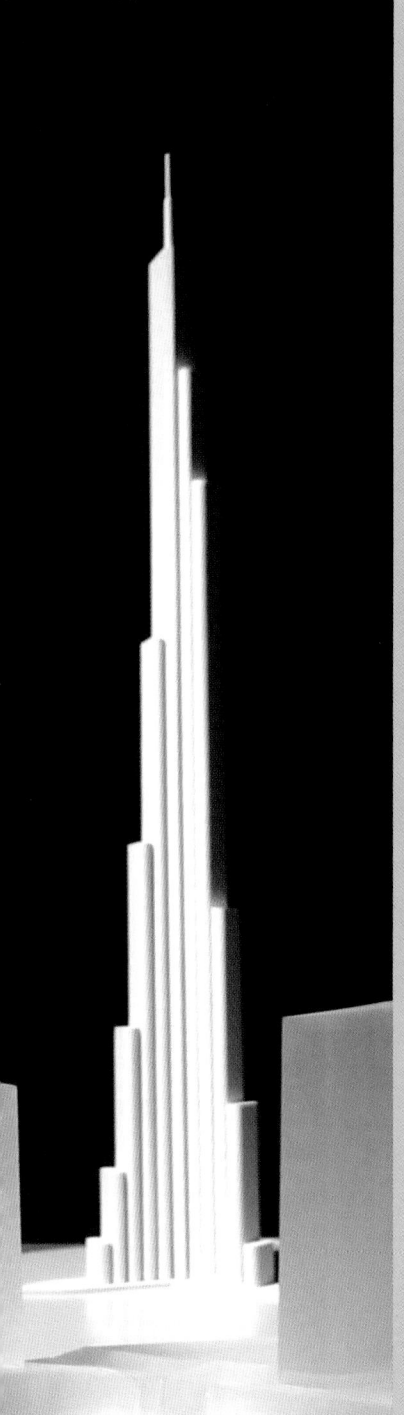

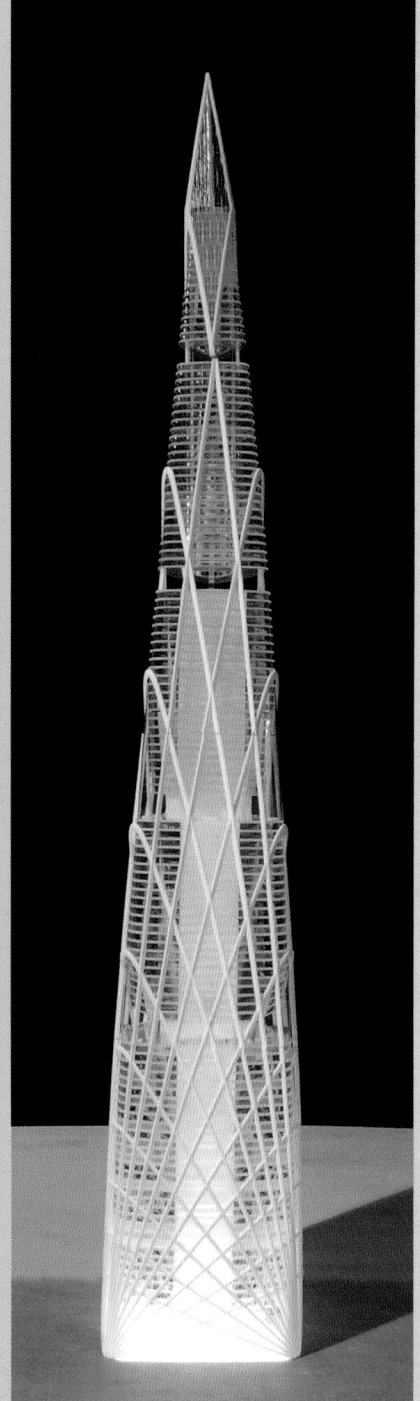

Office Tower

...edas 1:1000

Shanghai World Financial Centre

Pudong, Shanghai, PRC
KPF 1:1000 2002

Shanghai Centre

Pudong, Shanghai, PRC
Foster + Partners 1:500 2006

Macau Airport

Terminal Building, exploded view
1:200 1990

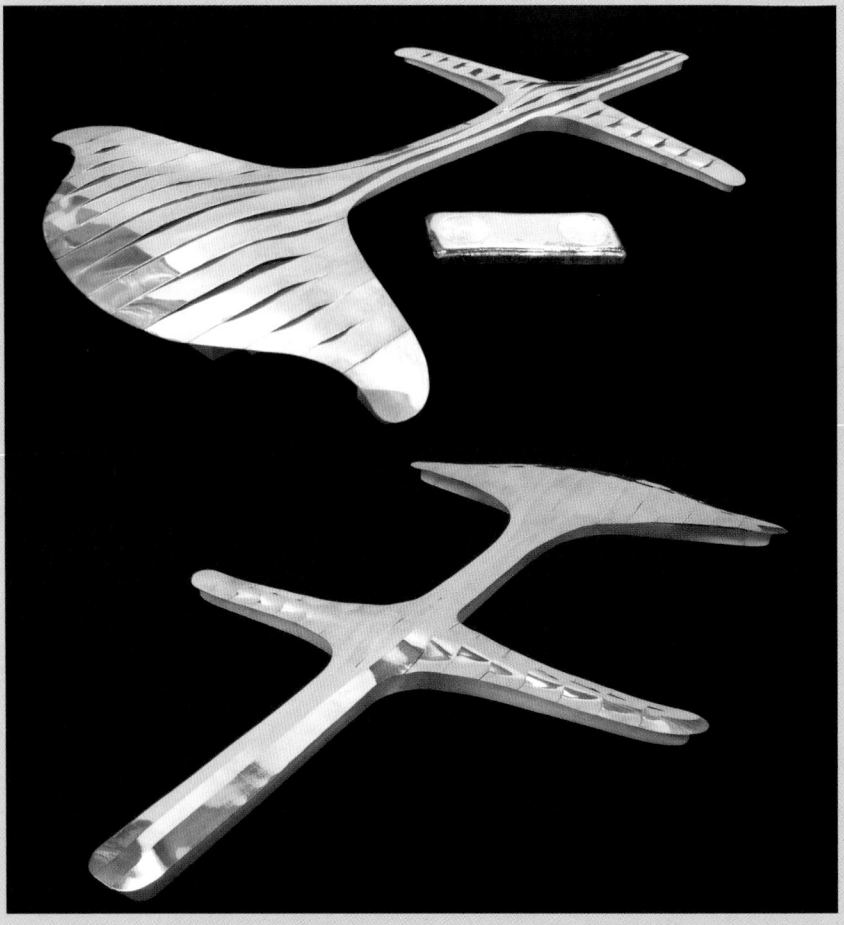

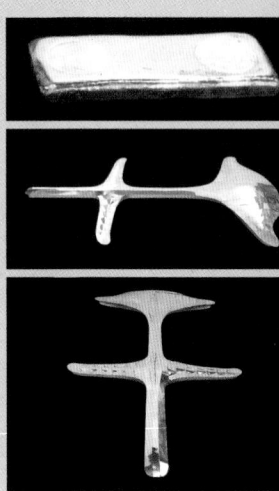

Shenzhen Airport

Terminal Building - competition model
(in solid silver)
Shenzhen, PRC
Foster + Partners 1:2000 2007

Foster + Partners wanted a model
with a metallic finish, not a spray
finish. I had only one week to make
the model. I chose silver because it is
malleable, easy to solder and can be
polished to a high sheen. I rolled-out
two solid ten-tael (750 grams) silver
bars to complete this model.

Seoul Airport

Terminal Building study model
Korea
HOK 1992

1:1000

Chubu Airport

2-bay Centre Concourse
Japan
HOK 1:100 2000

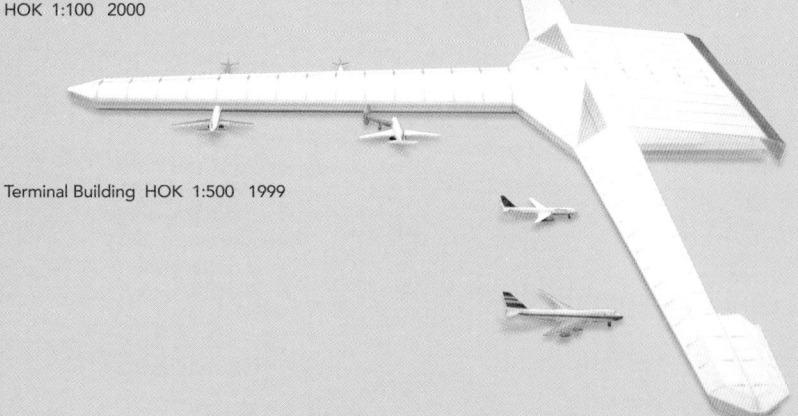

Terminal Building HOK 1:500 1999

Interiors

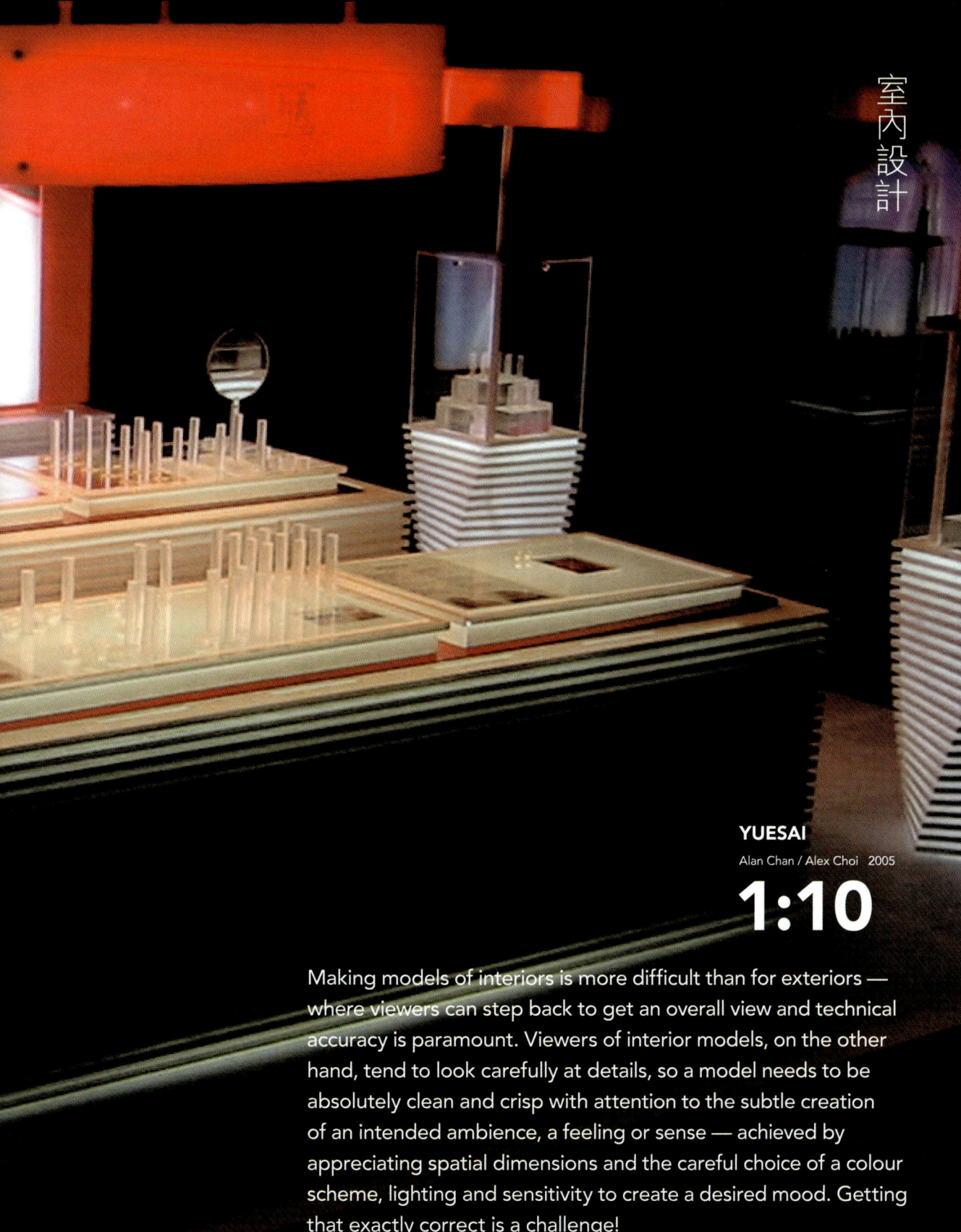

YUESAI

Alan Chan / Alex Choi   2005

1:10

Making models of interiors is more difficult than for exteriors —
where viewers can step back to get an overall view and technical
accuracy is paramount. Viewers of interior models, on the other
hand, tend to look carefully at details, so a model needs to be
absolutely clean and crisp with attention to the subtle creation
of an intended ambience, a feeling or sense — achieved by
appreciating spatial dimensions and the careful choice of a colour
scheme, lighting and sensitivity to create a desired mood. Getting
that exactly correct is a challenge!

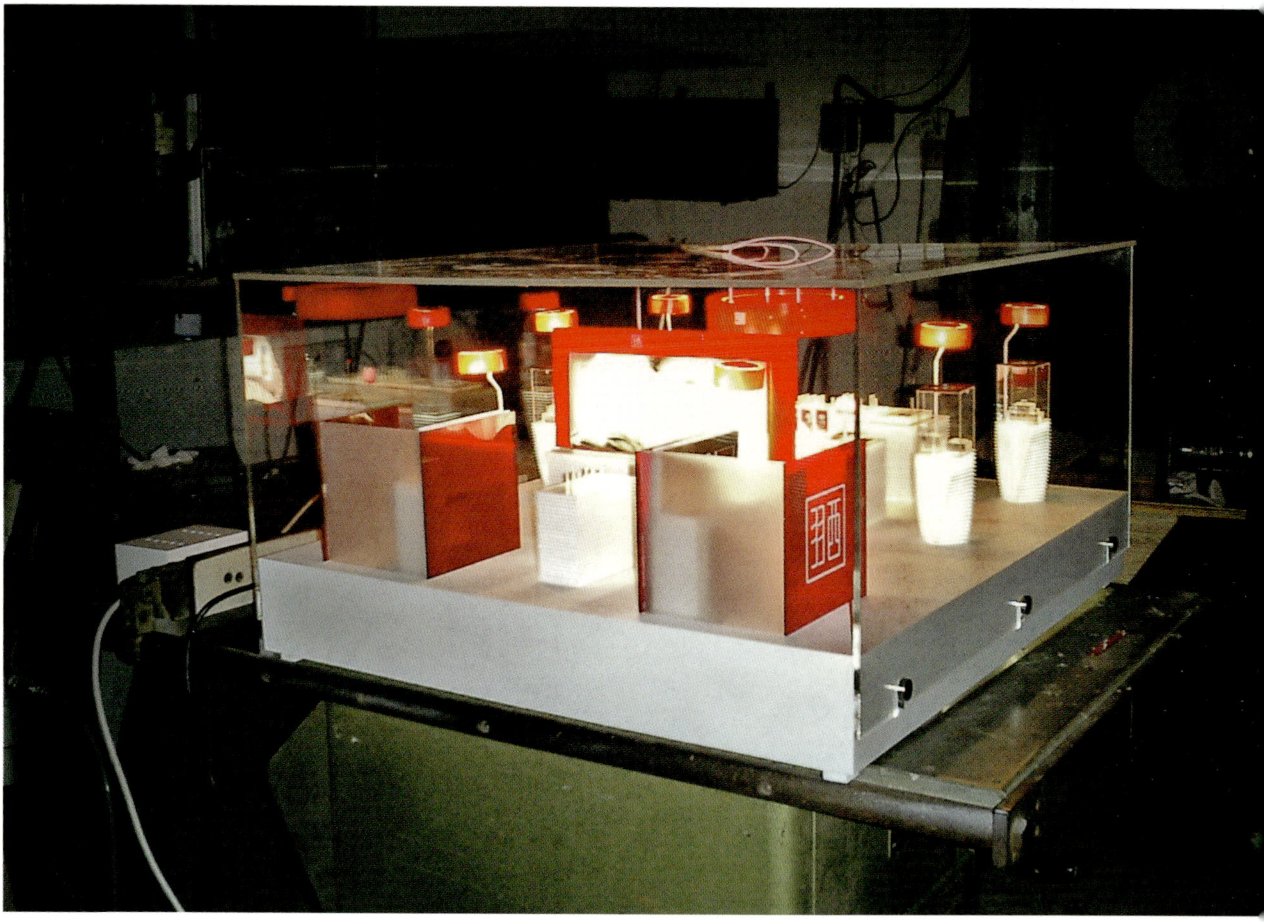

YUESAI

Hong Kong SAR
Alan Chan / Alex Choi 1:10 2005

Sample Boards and Box

Cathay Pacific Lounge
Hong Kong International Airport
Foster + Partners 2008

Hong Kong Handover

Exhibition Hall model
Hong Kong SAR
Pico 1:100 1997

An exhibition hall was set up in the new
wing of the Hong Kong Convention
and Exhibition Centre to celebrate the
return of Hong Kong's sovereignty to
China.

Innovation 2000

Exhibition Hall model
Hong Kong SAR
Pico 1:75 1999

Chater House

Shop front
Hong Kong SAR
Hongkong Land
LPT 1:20 2000

Chater House shop layout
LPT 1:20 2001

Sailing Ships

帆
船

Authentic Shipmodels Amsterdam

1977-1982

In partnership with Haring Piebenga of Authentic Shipmodels Amsterdam, we started a small production line making high quality handcrafted old sailing ships. Haring provided all the drawings and we provided a team of model makers in our workshop. We made 10-20 ships of the same model per run to cover our research and associated costs. Quality materials were used, including wood selected for its fine grain, specially woven ropes and hand cast cannons.

1 Three-mast sailing boat 1977-1982

2 Details of rigging 1977-1982
3 Details of sails and rigging 1977-1982

4 Details of battleship gun deck 1977-1982

1 Dutch leisure yacht 1977-1982
2 Two Mast Dutch sailing boat 1977-1982
3 Fujiang sea-going junk 1990
4 Hong Merchant's boat 1990

Product Design
Prototypes and Metalwork

Pacific Design

1:1   1982-1989

Pacific Design, headed by Kent Shimasaki and Dennis Chan, was the leading
freelance design company in Hong Kong during the 1980s. We were doing so
much work for Pacific Design that we were frequently chasing our own tails!
Their innovative designs and demand for high quality was a significant factor in
motivating us to improve our own modelling standards.

On the device face:

SCALE
FM 88 92 96 100 104 108 MHz
AM 70 95 120 160 UT

Products shown in the
following pages are
prototypes or hand-samples.

Z™

Z™ was created by New Horizons Product Development Company, and is the beginning of a series in life style products for both home and office use.

The philosophy behind Z™ is to create modern designs with an international appeal, which can be sold at prices that are economical to the average consumer.

This present collection features table top products in the areas of lighting, audio and stationery. Other ranges that will be available soon will include products in travel, healthcare and the outdoors.

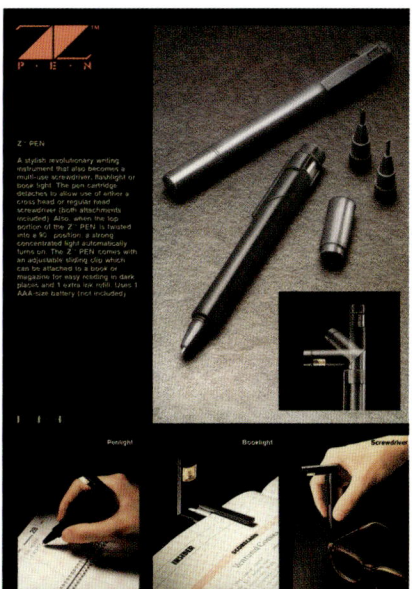

Z PEN

A stylish revolutionary writing instrument that also becomes a multi-use screwdriver, flashlight or book light. The pen cartridge detaches to allow use of either a cross head or regular head screwdriver (both attachments included). Also, when the top portion of the Z PEN is twisted into a 90° position, a strong concentrated light automatically turns on. The Z PEN comes with an adjustable sliding clip which can be attached to a book or magazine for easy reading in dark places and 1 extra ink refill. Uses 1 AAA-size battery (not included).

Penlight   Booklight   Screwdriver

DESK ACCESSORIES

Z PAD
A beautiful desk blotter from the Z collection of desk accessories. It's striking design is enhanced by the compartments engineered to hold other Z accessories.

Z TEL
The perfect desk or bedside telephone accessory, the Z Tel is a stylish, high-tech telephone index directory with a built-in telephone amplifier. It's patented design allows you to easily find a phone number in the office. For conference calls, simply attach the Z Tel's suction cup to the hand set and listen to the other party through the built-in speakers. A great executive or student gift or promotional item.

Z DECISION MAKER
And now, the perfect gift for the busy executive. Simply pose any yes or no question to the Z Decision Maker and it's built-in computer will instantly provide 1 of 6 answers on the display screen. The Z Decision Maker also comes with a memo pad and distinctive writing pen.

Z ORGANIZER

Now you can organize all of your writing instruments, notes, envelopes, rubber bands, paper clips (the well is magnetic), etc. in an attractive and modern styled desk sculpture. The Z Organizer's 2 sections can be twisted to suit your needs or desires without ever interfering with its function. In addition to these features, it also contains a pop-out jumbo digital clock with day date.

Z LITE

This is a unique desk lamp which can be sculpted to various angles and shapes. Utilizing a new patented process, the UL-approved Z Lite uses no wires in the main body, which enables safe and easy twisting. Comes with an extra-long 12 foot coil cord.

Z CLOCK RADIO

From the exciting Z designer's collection comes the ultimate AM/FM clock radio. The Z Clock Radio features a quartz accurate digital LED clock with dimmer switch, wakes you with an alarm or your radio, snooze, slide volume control and directional speaker. In addition, it has a built-in soft night light which can be directed to almost any position. It's unique patented design will make it one of the most popular consumer products for years to come.

Photographs of prototypes are often used in brochures before the actual product comes off the production line – to save time!

216

Pacific Design 1982-1989

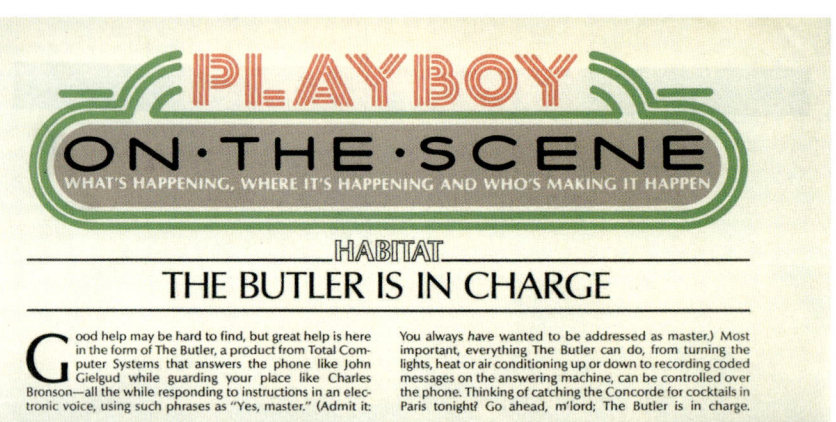

PLAYBOY
ON·THE·SCENE
WHAT'S HAPPENING, WHERE IT'S HAPPENING AND WHO'S MAKING IT HAPPEN

HABITAT
THE BUTLER IS IN CHARGE

Good help may be hard to find, but great help is here in the form of The Butler, a product from Total Computer Systems that answers the phone like John Gielgud while guarding your place like Charles Bronson—all the while responding to instructions in an electronic voice, using such phrases as "Yes, master." (Admit it:

You always *have* wanted to be addressed as master.) Most important, everything The Butler can do, from turning the lights, heat or air conditioning up or down to recording coded messages on the answering machine, can be controlled over the phone. Thinking of catching the Concorde for cocktails in Paris tonight? Go ahead, m'lord; The Butler is in charge.

Below: Even Bertie Wooster's Jeeves couldn't remember the phone numbers of 75 of his closest friends, and that's just one of The Butler's minor accomplishments, as this gentlemen's gentleman does everything to keep your household running smoothly, from automatically calling the police/fire department (and reporting the emergency via your recorded voice) or making a prerecorded call at a time you select to controlling up to 50 lamp and appliance outlets to making tea or even minding the temperature of the wine cellar. All for $699, plus $12.95 per extra module, by Total Computer Systems Inc., Newport, Rhode Island. A very good buy, sir. Now, if we could just teach it how to make a dry martini. . . .

JIM IMBROGNO

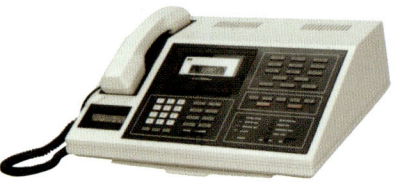

The making of a prototype is an integral part of product design. A prototype of a product or object is built before tooling starts, ensuring that all components can be accommodated into a product's available space; and, ensuring that parts can be assembled and disassembled easily and that there is enough ventilation for heat generated by electronic components. Key questions that a designer considers at the prototype stage of product development include: is it user friendly? Is it ergonomically comfortable? Colour scheme? Testing of most aspects of a product prototype, except a drop test, can be done and improved at this stage.

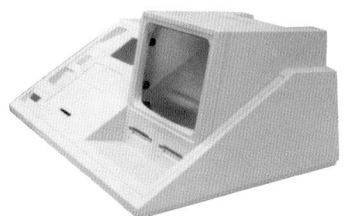

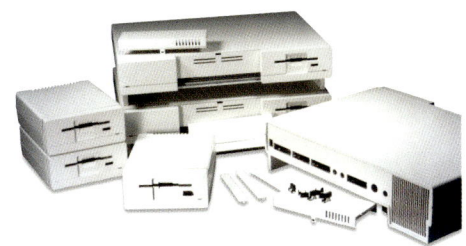

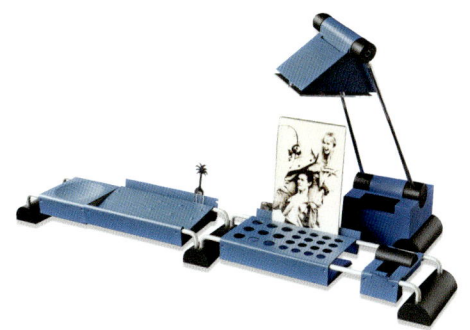

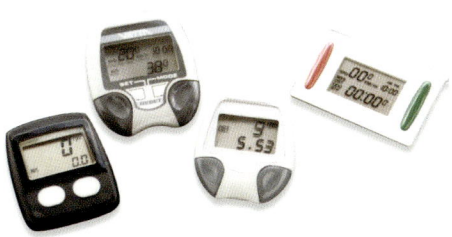

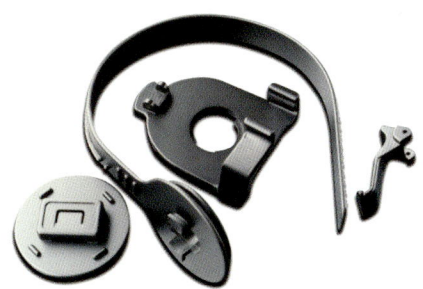

New Horizons / Pacific Design 1982-1989

1/2 Car tooling model Herpa 1:12 1987-1989
  3 Tooling model Herpa / Hogan 1:100 1987
  4 Hand-sample Herpa / Hogan 1:200 1987
  5 Hand-sample Herpa / Hogan 1:200 1987
  6 Tooling model Herpa / Hogan 1:100 1987-198

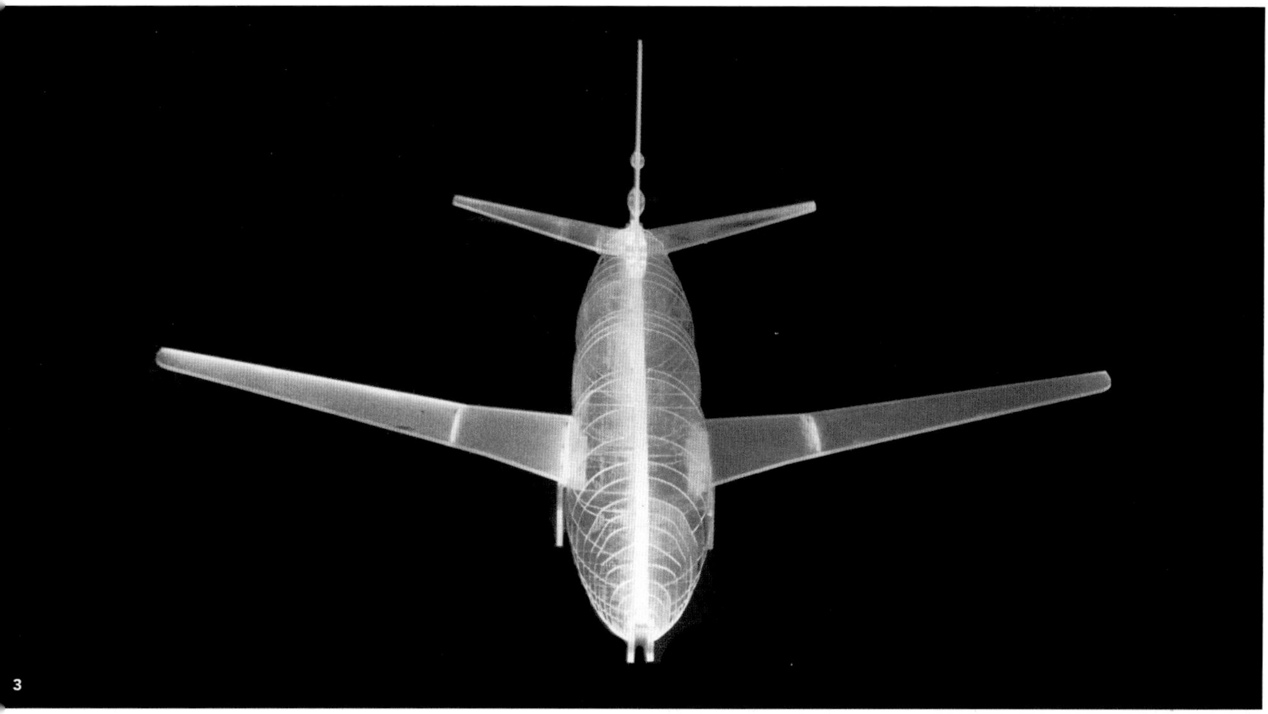

3

Herpa was the leading scale car model manufacturer in Germany and wanted to break into the scale airplane model market. We were asked by them to make a prototype of an airplane, which was later shown to Lufthansa as a sale sample.

4

5

6

Bronze and Silver Casting

Working in conjunction with Haring Piebenga
of Authentic Shipmodels Amsterdam,
Andre Lassen is a sculptor who designs
gift and decorative items, such as sundials,
to complement the company's main ship
model product lines. We cast many bronze
miniatures and items of silver jewellery from
Andre's designs.

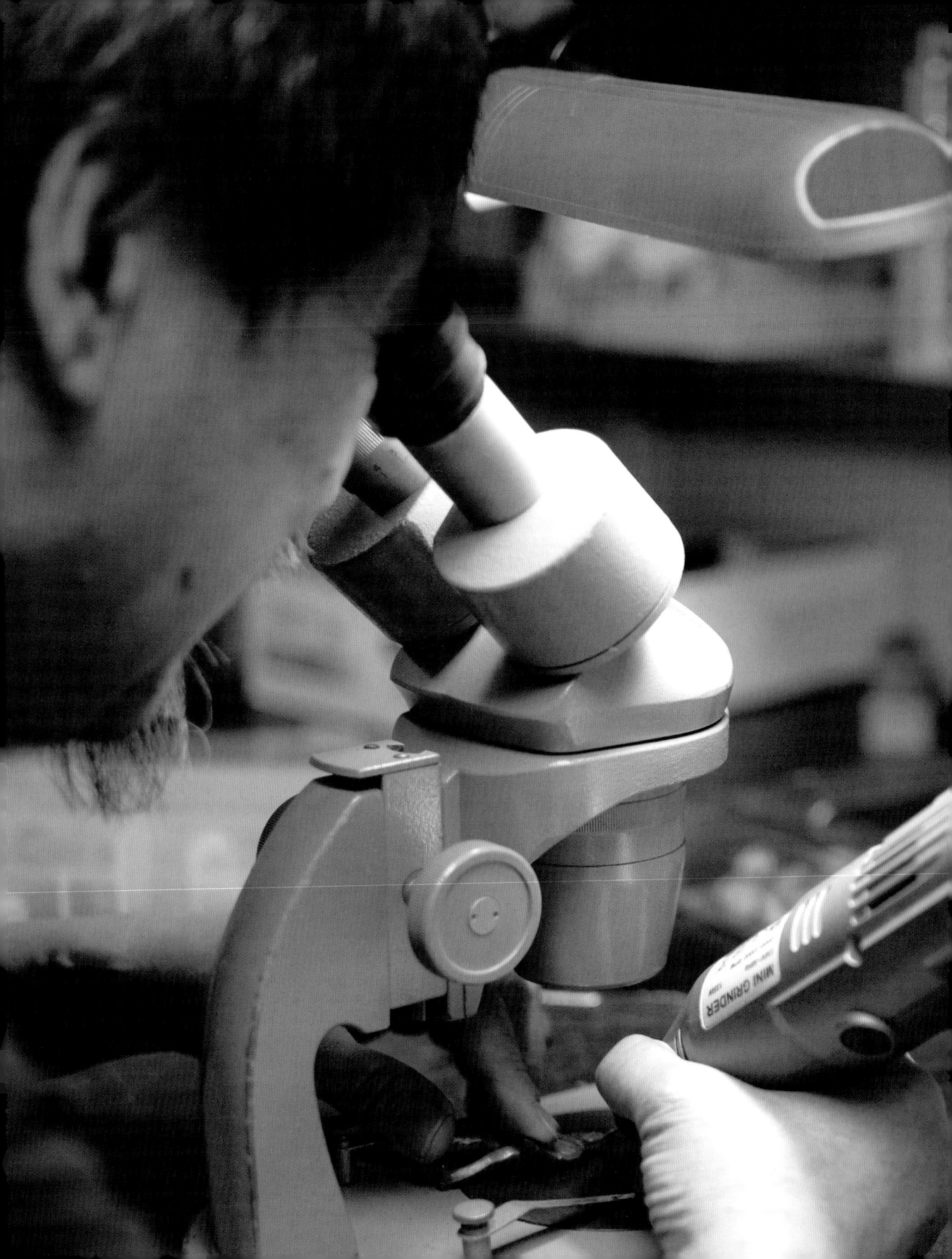

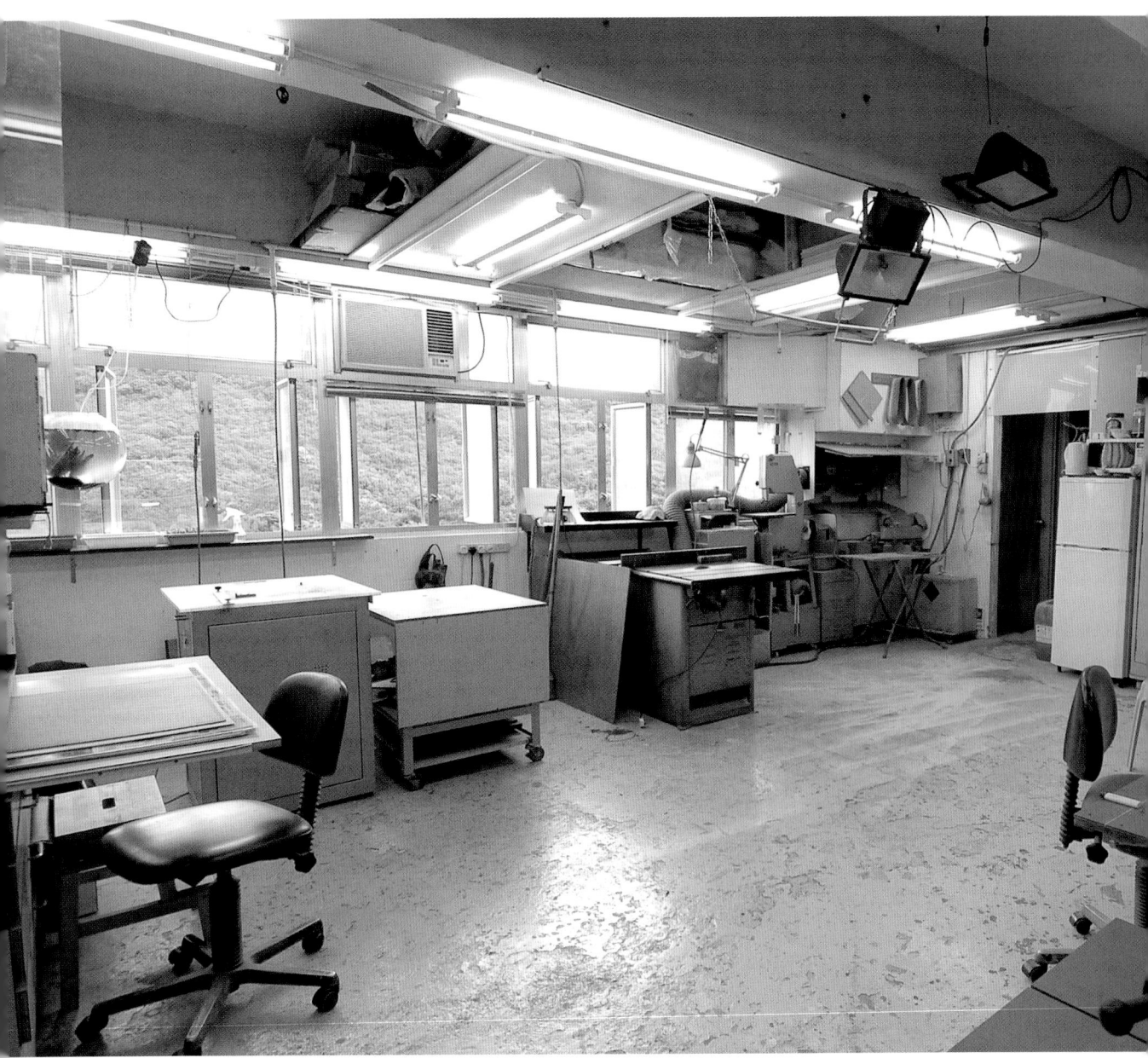

My Workshop

工作室

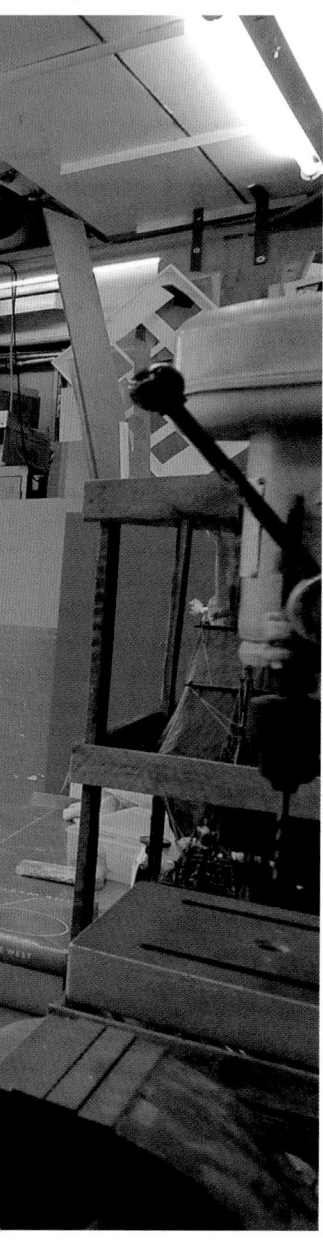

For a model maker, having an effective and efficient workshop is very important. My workshop is an extension of my home; in fact I spend more time in my workshop than at home. I acquired my current workshop in 1984, and considerable thought has gone into its design and layout. It has a highly flexible layout to accommodate different sized models and most of the machines and worktops are on wheels so that they can be pushed around to form different configurations as required.

I believe that a workshop must be clean, efficiently laid out and have plenty of elbowroom. On one side of my workshop, there is a bank of windows which provide good ventilation and natural light, both of which are important for colour fixing. Every two metres along each wall of the workshop are electric power points and pressurised air supply outlets. The workshop also has a 3-phase electricity supply for the industrial machines that we use.

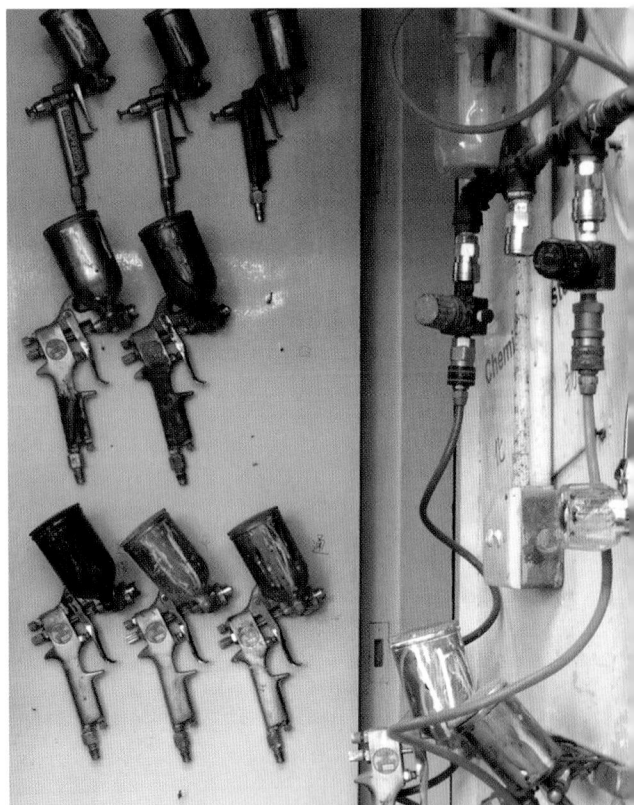

I believe in using good quality machines and tools — they might
be more expensive to buy, but they are a pleasure to use. I insist
upon them all being kept well maintained and in good order. The
workshop has a circular saw, a band saw, a jig saw, a drill press, a
large lathe, a small lathe and various routers. In addition, there is
a vacuum pump for vacuum forming and silicone mould casting,
and most importantly, computers and a laser-cutting machine.

We maintain an inventory of materials as we cannot go shopping every time we start a project. We have acrylic sheets in various thicknesses, from 0.5mm to 75mm, acrylic rods, acrylic tubes, brass rods, metal tubes, aluminium angles, many varieties of wood, screws and nuts, halogen lights, fluorescent tubes, LEDs, wires in different colours and gauges, transformers, timers, switches, human figures and cars in different scales, and a variety of trees in assorted shapes, sizes and colours.

We have dedicated spray guns for each of the primary and secondary colours and for the neutral colours, plus a range of paints enabling us to mix other colours as required. Sometimes, it is not possible for us to mix the required colour and when this happens we call up the ICI agent, give them either the ICI colour code number or the Pantone number and let them mix the paint for us.

Each different type of material and small tool has its own pigeon hole. In this way, everyone knows where to look for what he needs, and where to put things back when he has finished. However, this is easier said than done, especially when faced with tight deadlines; so, after a major project, we have a big clean up and put everything back where it belongs, ready for the next project.

I always like to take photographs of the models we make in order to keep a record of the model and for future reference. However, there is usually very little time for these photographs to be taken between finishing the model and its delivery. Therefore, in the workshop we have readily available photographic lights and different backdrops mounted from the ceiling which can be pulled down quickly for a photo-shoot. When we are really pushed for time photographers and architects often come with their equipment to take photographs in our workshop. In this case, they usually give me the slides of their shots or I mount my camera on their already setup tripod and take the photograph myself. Once a model is finished and delivered, the only memory that remains is the slides, negatives and photographs.

Acknowledgements

Portrait by Pottery Chan

I thank and am indebted to many colleagues, friends and family, without whose help this book and all the models seen here could not have been completed.

First, I thank all my colleagues at 3D Models, especially the model makers, who worked with me over many years to realise the vision of designers and architects and helped build these beautiful models: Mike Leung Hing Kwong, Au Yeung Tin Choi, Chu Pui Yin, Leung King To, Au Yeung Tin Shum, Raymond Kwok Wai Kui, So Kin Wing, Wong Tung Pang, Cheung Ling Fung, Brian Yam Lap Yin, and also my personal assistant, Au May Ling, who does all the things I hate to do – processing the inevitable administrative and financial paperwork, answering the phone and paying the bills.

In addition, I also want to thank Haring Piebenga of Authentic Shipmodels Amsterdam who gave me financial support and the opportunity to evolve from a one-man model making operation to a full-sized well equipped model workshop.

I am equally grateful to the many designers and architects who, over the last 36 years, have entrusted me with their beloved projects, and worked closely with me to successfully deliver each of the models. In particular Keith Griffiths and Andrew Bromberg of Aedas; Steve McKelvey of Architects Pacific; Lambert Heuvelmans of Ferrero; Ian Lambot, Alex Lifschutz, Roy Fleetwood, Kent Lui, Chris Seddon, Mouzhan Majidi, Winston Shu and Richard Hawkins of Foster + Partners;

鳴
謝

Lucy Chui of Greensward; Anthony Hackett of Hackett and Griffiths; Paul Wong of Hogan; Ernest Cirangle and Tom Boshaw of HOK; Clive Miners of Miners Models; Wong Kam Pui of Opal; Dennis Chan and Kent Shimasaki of Pacific Design; Anthony Rastrick and Scott Findley of RMJM; Eric Carlsen of Topper Toys; and, Alan Macdonald of Urbis.

I also want to acknowledge the contribution of the photographers, architects and model makers who took or provided photographs and graphics contained in the 3D Models archive, from which this book was compiled, and the designers and graphic designers, in particular Dennis S.L. Chan, who helped me with the initial layout of the book.

I want to thank my mother, who, although uneducated, was a free thinker and believed we should do whatever we were best at; and, my father, who by example, showed his children not to be afraid of hard work or adversity; he believed that you could learn about most things from a book; and, also my uncles Lee Loong and Cheng Sui from whom I learnt a lot when I was a child. I would like to express my lasting gratitude to my elder brother Po, who has given me constant encouragement and support throughout my life; and, my younger brother Wai, who comes to my workshop in his free time to keep me company and to restore various parts for his antique cars.

And finally, my very special thanks to my daughter Katherine and my son William, for putting up with my long hours of work and to my wife Jane, who encouraged me to start my own business and helped me to set it up, and whose steadfast support has enabled me to turn my enjoyable hobby into a wonderful and fulfilling work life.

Photography and Graphic Credits

Page	Frame	Source / Photographer	Page	Frame	Source / Photographer
004/005		J.Fung	066/067		K.Y.Chung
006/007		J.Fung	068/069	1-3	K.Y.Chung
010		3D Models	070/071	1/2	K.Y.Chung
014/015	1-3/5-10/12-14	3D Models	072/073	1-5	K.Y.Chung
	4	Clare Grinsell	075		K.Y.Chung
	11	Foster Ass. HK - KJAW	076/077	1-6	K.Y.Chung
016/017	1-4/7-10/12/16-17	3D Models	078/079		K.Y.Chung
	5	Hackett & Griffiths - KJAW	080/081	1/2	K.Y.Chung
	6/11/13-15	K.Ip	082/083	1-3	K.Y.Chung
018/019	1-3/6-8/10-14	3D Models	084/085		K.Y.Chung
	4-5	K.Ip	086/087	1-5	K.Y.Chung
	9	K.Y.Tsai	088/089		K.Y.Chung
020/021	1/2/6-9	3D Models	090/091	1-3	K.Y.Chung
	3-5	K.Ip	092/093		LPT / K.Ip
	10	J.Fung	094/095	1/2	K.Y.Chung
022/023		Foster Ass. HK - KJAW	097		RMJM / K.Ip
024/025	1/2	KJAW	099		K.Y.Chung
026/027	1-5	KJAW	100/101		K.Y.Chung
028/029		KJAW	102/103	1-4	K.Y.Chung
030/031		Foster Ass. HK - KJAW	104/105	1-5	K.Y.Chung
032/033	1	Foster Ass. HK - KJAW	106/107	1	RMJM
	2	K.Y.Chung		2/5	RMJM / K.Ip
034/035	1	Foster Ass. HK - KJAW		3	Hackett & Griffiths / K.Ip
	2-7	K.Y.Chung		4	Hackett & Griffiths
036/037	1/2/4/9/10	Foster Ass. HK	108/109	1/2	K.Y.Chung
	3/5-8	KJAW		3/4	K.Y.Tsai
038/039	1/2/4-9	KJAW	110/111		K.Y.Chung
	3	Foster Ass. HK / Ian Lambot	112/113	1/3/4	Aedas / K.Ip
040/041		HOK / K.Ip		2	K.Y.Chung
042/043	1-3	K.Y.Chung	114/115	1/2	Aedas / K.Ip
044/045	1/3/4	Foster Asia - KJAW	116	1/2	K.Y.Chung
	2	K.Y.Chung	117	1-11	K.Y.Chung
046/047	1-4	K.Y.Chung	118/119		K.Y.Chung
048	1	K.Y.Chung	120/121	1/2	Hackett & Griffiths
	2-4	KJAW	122/123	1-7	K.Y.Chung
049	1-4	K.Y.Chung	125	1/2	K.Y.Chung
050/051	1/2/5/6	Foster Asia - KJAW	127		K.Y.Chung
	3/4/7/8	K.Y.Chung	128/129	1-4	K.Y.Chung
052/053	Background	MTR	130-131		3D Models
	Train	K.Y.Chung	133	1/2	3D Models
054/055	1-7	KJAW	134/135	1-3	K.Y.Chung
056/057	1-5	K.Y.Chung	136/137	1-5	K.Y.Chung
058/059	1-6	K.Y.Chung	138/139	1/3	K.Y.Chung
060/061	1-7	K.Y.Chung		2	Hong Kong Museum of Art
062/063	1-6	K.Y.Chung	140/141		RMJM / K.Ip
064/065	1/2	Hackett & Griffiths - KJAW	142/143		J.Fung
	3	K.Y.Chung	145	1/2	K.Y.Chung

Page	Frame	Source / Photographer
146/147		J.Fung
148/149		K.Y.Chung
150/151		K.Y.Chung
152/153	1/2	K.Y.Chung
154/155	1-4	K.Y.Chung
156/157	1-3	Hackett & Griffiths
	4/5	K.Y.Chung
158		K.Y.Chung
161		K.Y.Chung
162	1	SOM - LPT
	2	K.Y.Chung
163	1-3	K.Y.Chung
164/165	1-3	Hackett Design / K.Ip
166/167	1/2	HOK / K.Ip
168/169	1-3	HOK / K.Ip
170/171	1-3	HOK - 3D Models
172/173	1/2	ArcPac / K.Ip
174	1/2	TaoHo Design - KJAW
175	1	CTB / K.Ip
	2	K.Y.Chung
176/177	1/2/4/7-10/12	K.Y.Chung
	3/5/6/11	K.Ip
178/179	1/2	K.Y.Chung
180/181	1/2	K.Y.Chung
182		HOK / K.Ip
183		K.Y.Chung
184/185	1	HOK / K.Ip
	2-5	K.Y.Chung
186		M.Au
187		3D Models
188/189	1	K.Y.Chung
	2	K.Y.Tsai
190/191	1/2/4	Aedas / K.Ip
	3	K.Y.Chung
192/193	1-3	K.Y.Chung
194/195	1-8	K.Y.Chung
196/197	1-3/5/6	K.Y.Chung
	4	HOK / K.Ip
198/199		K.Y.Chung
200/201	1-4	K.Y.Chung
202/203	1-3	K.Y.Chung
204	1-2	K.Y.Chung
206/207		3D Models
208/209	1-4	3D Models
210/211	1-4	3D Models
212		Pacific Design
213		K.Y.Chung

Page	Frame	Source / Photographer
214/215	1-7	Pacific Design
216/217	1	PLAYBOY
	2-10	3D Models
218/219		3D Models
220/221	1-6	K.Y.Chung
222		K.Y.Chung
223		M.Au
224/225		J.Fung
226/227		J.Fung
228/229		K.Y.Chung
230/231	1-4	K.Y.Chung
232/233	1-8	M.Au
234	1-2	M.Au
236		P.Chan

Cover photo: M.Au

The models pictured in this book were made in Hong Kong by King Y. Chung and his KJAW / 3D Models team except for a small number — about 3% — made in conjunction with the architect / architect's model maker.

Every reasonable attempt has been made to identify owners of copyright. Errors or omissions will be corrected in subsequent editions.